AMBUSHED!

AMBUSHED!

A Cartoon History of the George W. Bush Administration

JIM MORIN *and* WALTER C. CLEMENS, JR.

Paradigm Publishers
Boulder • London

Jim Morin's cartoons are distributed internationally by the Cartoonists and Writers Syndicate
67 Riverside Drive
New York, NY 10024

Published in the United States by Paradigm Publishers, 3360 Mitchell Lane Suite E, Boulder, CO 80301 USA.

Paradigm Publishers is the trade name of Birkenkamp & Company, LLC, Dean Birkenkamp, president and publisher.

Library of Congress Cataloging-in-Publication Data
Morin, Jim.
Ambushed! : a cartoon history of the George W. Bush administration / Jim Morin and Walter C. Clemens, Jr.
p.   cm.
Includes bibliographical references and index.
ISBN 978-1-59451-582-8 (pbk. : alk. paper)
1. United States—Politics and government—2001– 2. United States—Politics and government—2001—Caricatures and cartoons. 3. Bush, George W. (George Walker), 1946– 4. Bush, George W. (George Walker), 1946—Caricatures and cartoons. 5. American wit and humor, Pictorial. I. Clemens, Walter C. II. Title.
E902.M67   2008
973.93—dc22
2008023691

Printed and bound in the United States of America on acid free paper that meets the standards of the American National Standard for Permanence of Paper for Printed Library Materials.

Designed and typeset by Jane Raese

13 12 11 10 09 08 1 2 3 4 5

TRAVELING through England at the time of King Arthur, a visitor from nineteenth-century America asked some "ostensible freemen … if they supposed a nation of people ever existed, who, with a free vote in every man's hand, would elect that a single family and its descendants should reign over it forever, whether gifted or boobies, to the exclusion of all other families. …

"They all looked unhit, and said they didn't know; and that they had never thought about it before, and it hadn't ever occurred to them that a nation could be so situated that every man could have a say in the government. … But presently one man looked up and asked me to state that proposition again; and state it slowly, so it could soak into his understanding. I did it; and after a little he had the idea, and he brought his fist down and said he didn't believe a nation where every man had a vote would involuntarily get down in the mud and dirt in any such way; and that to steal from a nation its will and preference must be a crime and the first of all crimes."

The visitor was from Connecticut, later the birthplace of George W. Bush, where the constitution holds "that all political power is inherent in the people, and all free governments are founded on their authority and instituted for their benefit."

The author of this tale, Mark Twain, believed that "the citizen who thinks he sees that the commonwealth's political clothes are worn out, and yet holds his peace and does not agitate for a new suit, is disloyal; he is a traitor." His kind of loyalty was to his country—"the real thing, the substantial thing, the eternal thing … the thing to watch over, and care for, and be loyal to."

—*A Connecticut Yankee in King Arthur's Court* (1889), chapter 13

Contents

Introduction

WHEN GEORGE W. BUSH moved into the White House in 2001, many Americans looked forward to what they thought would be a new era of conservatism—one that the president called "compassionate conservatism." He promised a return to moral values, a humble foreign policy, and relief from big government. From its first days, however, the Bush administration rejected the July 4, 1776, admonition of the Founding Fathers to observe a "decent respect to the opinions of mankind." But when terrorists struck on September 11, 2001, most Americans applauded the president's commitment to wage a "war on terror"—without help

from others, if need be. When the Bush team shocked and awed the world by a blitz into Saddam Hussein's lair, many Americans rejoiced that their country moved decisively without waiting for approval by the miscreants at the United Nations.

Seven years later, however, most Americans thought the United States had moved in the wrong direction since 2001. Republicans led by John McCain as well as Democrat followers of Barack Obama demanded "change."

People around the world also hoped that the next presidency would be different. They could not vote in U.S. elections but their lives—even their weather, their

food intake, and their security—would be shaped by the forty-fourth president and his administration.

Our book recalls what happened and what went wrong—at home and abroad—under the forty-third president, George W. Bush. The looming pitfalls were evident from the beginning—a forced entry into the White House arranged by Florida's secretary of state and five Supreme Court justices, an all-out campaign to cut taxes for the rich, a rejection of environmental safeguards, and an "unsigning" of the statute founding the International Criminal Court. Having trashed the basics of democracy in the United States, the Bush team lacked

credibility when, later, it preached free elections and the rule of law to Afghanis and Iraqis.

At the same time, Americans and the world got a gang that couldn't shoot straight, as we are reminded by the cartoon that opens Chapter 1 of this book. The Bush administration proved to be as ineffective as it was deceitful. Some top dogs in the Bush gang liked to hunt. Sometimes they hit their target—sometimes not. The Vice, aka Dick Cheney, shot his hunting partner in February 2006, presumably by accident. What was notable was not that he failed to hit his real target but that, as happened often, both Cheney and his nominal boss, George W. Bush, tried to keep this incident from public knowledge and scrutiny.

Incompetence and deception became the rule throughout the eight years when the Bush gang held and pulled the levers of power. Often they shot at the wrong target; often they missed. But they were almost never straight shooters—almost never explained what they were really doing or why. More often than not, they used sweet talk and half-truths to mask their ambitions and operations. Sometimes they outright lied—as detailed in the memoir of Bush's longtime press secretary, Scott McClellan.

Neither creator of this book has been a dogmatic partisan of either party. For decades each of us has pointed out what we saw as the foibles and follies of Democrats as well as Republicans. We hope to do so in the years ahead. Jim Morin was born in the home state of the Adams family— Samuel, John, and John Quincy, as well as the Kennedy tribe. But Walter Clemens came from a citadel of conservatism: the hometown of William Howard and Robert A. Taft, located in a state long represented by Senator John W. Bricker.

We would prefer to cheer than to castigate our leaders, but we must call a spade a spade. As Mark Twain put it, "A discriminating irreverence is the creator and protector of human liberty."

As a new millennium began, Clemens was completing a book surveying America's foreign policy achievements and failures since 1898. In the 1990s, it seemed to him, the United States was on the right course at home and abroad. This reverie was broken by the virtual coup d'état that handed the presidency to George W. Bush in November 2000. The

very first actions of the new administration spurred Clemens to write "How to Lose Friends and Inspire Enemies" for the Outlook section of the *Washington Post*. Soon he wrote another column for Outlook arguing that Bush violated the Constitution by abrogating the ABM treaty without congressional approval—an article that helped inspire thirty-three House members to sue the president.

While writing a broader survey of Bush's first term, Clemens found that Morin's political cartoons in the *Miami Herald* were dissecting the gap between Bush words and actions nearly every day. Our concerns and outlooks dovetailed. Morin's pictures, Clemens thought, were worth a thousand or more words. If we could combine images with political analysis, the result could be a powerful synergy. Our review of Bush's first term was called *Bushed! What Passionate Conservatives Have Done to America and the World* (2004). We try to continue this synergy in *Ambushed!*

Clemens believes his own work has been enriched by the ideas of colleagues at Boston University, Harvard University, and other institutions. For help on this book, he especially thanks Luke Rosseel, Laura d'Amore, and Sharon Donahue in Boston, and Jennifer Knerr at Paradigm Publishers in Boulder. Most of the facts presented in this book are drawn from documents and press reports easily found by searching the Web. Ideas on how they fit together are suggested in the books, articles, and government reports listed in the Relevant Readings section of this book. Of course divergent and opposed interpretations abound. See, for example, the 2008 anti-liberal treatise of Ben Stein, Fox News commentator, and Phil DeMuth, "advisor to high net worth individuals, institutions, and foundations," *How to Ruin the United States of America* (Carlsbad, CA: New Beginnings, 2008). What we try to offer, however, is not only a set of tragic truths but also many good laughs—a combination we hope may help to provoke actions that save America and humanity from ruin.

Jim Morin
Miami, Florida

Walter C. Clemens, Jr.
Lexington, Massachusetts

1

The Bush Gang

"Bad ideas have come and gone in American history. Rarely if ever though, has such a small band of misfits and hucksters done as much damage to the nation as the Bush crew."

—Sean Wilentz
professor of history, Princeton University, in *Rolling Stone*, May 4, 2006

HOW DID we get here? Was the American public ambushed by a gang that couldn't shoot straight? If the root of the word "ambush" refers to a hidden peril or trap—often from the bush or woods—we have to ask ourselves whether we might have seen it coming.

Americans had some warning how George W. Bush would act if he became president. His record over two terms as Texas governor was ominous:

- More death row executions than in any other state—150 in six years under Governor Bush, who granted clemency in just one case.
- Support for and signature on a 1995 law designed to limit

"THIS RIGHT TO LIFE CANNOT BE GRANTED OR DENIED BY GOVERNMENT BECAUSE IT DOES NOT COME FROM GOVERNMENT, IT COMES FROM *the* CREATOR OF LIFE."
— G.W. BUSH

TEXAS EXECUTIONS

NEXT!!

GOV

DEATH WARRANT

MORIN 9/17/03
The Miami Herald

appeals by death row inmates and shorten the time between conviction and execution.
• The lowest tax rates in the nation and among the lowest levels of public services.
• Inbreeding of energy businesses with government, with Enron providing the greatest subsidies for Bush's two runs for governor.
• Nothing but "voluntary" restraints on smokestack industry, helping Texas acquire

3

some of the dirtiest air in America.

- A façade of improved education based on standardized but relatively easy tests from which weaker students and delinquents were often excused.
- Reliance on faith-based institutions for social welfare.

The signs were that George W. and his political mastermind Karl Rove would stop at nothing to win an election. For Rove, politics is war by other means. A whisper campaign against Ann Richards (she befriends lesbians) helped Bush win the governor's mansion in 1994. A similar campaign against John McCain (said to be mentally unfit after Vietnam) helped Bush clinch the Republican nomination for presi-

dent in 2000. Reliance on the Big Lie—assertions so outlandish they must be true—became a hallmark of Bush politics.

Still, it was not clear how far

George W. Bush would carry over his Texas policies if he occupied the White House. Campaigning for president in 2000, he promised a "compassionate conservatism."

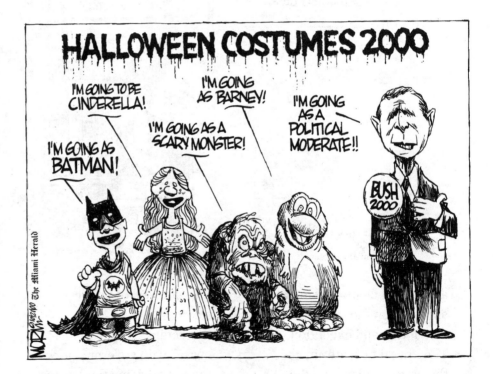

He called for a "humble" posture in world affairs and forswore efforts at "nation-building." Though admittedly callow in foreign policy, George W. was advised by an expert, Condoleezza Rice, who herself had been tutored by Brent Scowcroft, national security assistant to the 41st president, George W.'s father, and former Secretary of State George Shultz.

Personality and Politics

Even some of those who lauded Bush's Texas policies worried about the personal makeup of "Dubya." At Yale a C student, a draft-dodger in his twenties, an alcoholic in his thirties, a failed businessman rescued only by his father's connections, Dubya said that he stopped drinking at age forty and found Jesus. Some psychologists warned that recovered alcoholics and reborn Christians are prone to black-and-white thinking and sharp zigzags in their behavior. It seems more than a little ironic that Bush's latter day moralism coexisted with rampant corruption in his presidency and that many of its tenets flew in the face of traditional conservatism.

But does personality shape policy? Isn't the president limited by the Constitution? By the "separation of powers" that compels the president to partner with Congress under the watchful eye of the Supreme Court? By the process by which every initiative of the president and Congress is transformed as it passes through the federal and state bureaucracies?

Surely the answer to all these questions is *Yes*. The president *is* limited. But his or her personal makeup, ambitions, operational style, and chosen helpers all leave a deep impact on how America is governed, and these can ultimately be the biggest limitations of all. If Woodrow Wilson had been less dogmatic and more inclined to compromise, he could have secured Senate approval for the League of Nations. If Lyndon Johnson had not inherited Camelot and feared to deviate from the Kennedy legacy, he might well have cut short America's involvement in Vietnam.

Like Father, Like Son?

Some observers wondered whether, if George W. became

president, he would set his sights on finishing off the job his father left undone and try to knock Saddam Hussein from power in Baghdad. Some analysts correctly surmised that George W. would never make the policy switch—raising taxes—that helped kill his father's campaign for a second term.

But only intimates of the Bush and Walker families were aware of the contradictory impulses that drove father and son—the 41st and, later, the 43rd presidents of the United States. Both "Poppy" and George W. emerged from two very different family traditions. The elder George was an upright pillar of the community; the younger, a rowdy and vacuous playboy. As described by *Slate* editor Jacob Weisbert in *The Bush Tragedy*, the Bush side came

The World According to George W. Bush

The Miami Herald

from New England—Protestant and upper class, accustomed to having money and privilege but against shows of wealth and devoted to public service. The other side—the Walkers, Midwestern Catholics—sought money for its own sake and liked to flaunt it.

The 41st president made his own fortune in the oil fields but, having served bravely in World War II, spent most of his life in government service. By contrast, the 43rd president avoided military service; exploited his family ties to finance business ventures; and piggybacked on his father's reputation to win the Republican nomination for president in 2000.

Like father, unlike son? Probably things were not so simple. The elder Bush can also be seen as an intellectual cipher with a grubby streak. Estimates of payoffs by the Moonie Mafia to the ex-president and wife Barbara for publicly endorsing Moonie causes in Argentina and Japan range from one to ten million dollars. Of course not all men (and women) live by bread alone. For some people, ideas and ideals are paramount—even when they run contrary to narrow self-interest. The Roosevelt, Rockefeller, and Kennedy dynasties produced

public-spirited leaders quite different from George W. and the other sons of George H. W. and Barbara—Jeb and Neil.

Having rarely traveled outside the United States and known for spending an inordinate amount of time at his Texas ranch, George W. Bush entered into the American presidency at just the point the United States was thrust most decidedly—and devastatingly—onto the world stage.

George W. wanted to be different from his father and to outdo younger brother Jeb, on whom the family had placed its highest hopes. Although Poppy tended to be moderate and cautious, George W. tended to be radical and bold. Where George H. W. Bush carried a broad foreign policy experience into an engagement with world affairs, George W. thumbed his nose at the world and practiced a unilateral, isolating foreign policy.

The Rest of the Gang

When George W. Bush became president, his penchant for bold behavior was encouraged by Vice President Dick Cheney, who was determined since Watergate to strengthen the institution of president. Cheney was pivotal also in bringing fellow hardliners into the foreign policy apparatus of the 43rd president: Donald Rumsfeld, Paul Wolfowitz, Douglas Feith, John Bolton, and others. Whereas President Ronald Reagan used neoconservatives, the "neocons" used George W. Bush. Although the president was not attracted to intellectuals and their theorizing,

The Miami Herald

9

the advisers surrounding Bush managed to put their ideas in policy terms that facilitated an alliance of foreign policy hawks, Christian conservatives, the Israel lobby, and the military-congressional-industrial complex. George W. counted on this band to help him avoid the mistakes that made his father a one-term president. The result was two terms of bumbling, bald-faced lies, and bellicosity.

Campaigns & Elections

Over that summer of 2002, top Bush aides ... outlined a strategy for carefully orchestrating the coming campaign to aggressively sell the war. ... In the permanent campaign era, it was all about manipulating sources of public opinion to the president's advantage.

—Scott McClellan
  press secretary to the Bush administration, in *What Happened: Inside the Bush White House and Washington's Culture of Deception* (2008)

CONSERVATIVES CLAIM to value patriotism more than liberals do, but nearly half the voters in 2000 and 2004 favored a "compassionate conservative" candidate who—quite unlike his father—had avoided active duty in wartime and failed to keep up even his minimal duties as a part-time pilot in the Air National Guard. Compounding these omissions, the Bush team proceeded to smear the reputations of two wartime heroes—John McCain in the 2000 primaries and John Kerry in the 2004 presidential campaign.

The Big Lie

To turn a campaign liability into an asset, the Bush public relations team generated one fictional biography of Bush and a second for his opponents. The smears against McCain and Kerry resembled those concocted by the Bush family and its advisers in races against Michael Dukakis in 1988, Ann Richards in 1994, and Max Cleland in Georgia's senate election of 2002. In 2004, the attack on John Kerry led to a new verb: "to swiftboat."

The swiftboat tack was "the total Rove package," said a

veteran observer of Texas politics, Lou Dubose. "When a race is close, launch a collateral attack against your opponent's greatest asset. . . . Keep your own candidate aloof from the controversy. Be persistent; if your opponent is explaining his position, he's losing. And leave no fingerprints."

15

Separation of Powers

Conservatives also claim to value law and order. They honor the Constitution and the separation of powers. But the Bush camp did not mind that Republican officials in Florida prevented many citizens from voting or expunged their votes in 2000 or that similar irregularities skewed the outcome in Ohio in 2004.

Al Gore won more popular votes than Bush in the November 2000 elections, but the outcome in the electoral college depended on the vote count in Florida, where George W.'s brother Jeb was governor. Florida's secretary of state, Katherine Harris, ruled on November 20, 2000, that George W. had won the state by 537 votes. But Democrats complained about many irregularities

such as the very confusing "butterfly ballot" used in largely Democratic Palm Beach County, where the votes of some thirty thousand persons were disqualified because they had "overvoted" or "undervoted."

In other Florida precincts voters were turned away because their names did not appear on a

The Miami Herald

master list that had not been up-dated. Blacks and Latinos complained they had been intimidated by police. About fifty thousand individuals, most of them likely to vote for Gore, were denied access to the polls in November 2000 because their names had been purged from Florida's list of eligible voters. The purge list was prepared by a private firm that later admitted making many errors, but explained that the list was supposed to be vetted by Florida authorities, who happened to be Republican.

Bush's team called for finality; Gore's, for fairness. Florida's secretary of state was hardly a model of impartiality, for Harris had *managed* the Bush campaign in the state! She pressed the Florida Supreme Court to halt manual recounts that had begun in several counties. But on November 21, the court ordered hand counts to continue, giving counties five days to complete them. When this deadline expired, Harris certified that Bush had won Florida's entire electoral vote. She turned away the results from Palm Beach County, which arrived two hours late. When Gore asked for a recount of some fourteen thousand undervotes, however, the Florida high court agreed. As Bush's lead slipped to 193 votes, his legal team asked the U.S. Supreme Court to halt the hand counting.

States' Rights

Conservatives claim to esteem states' rights, but Bush supporters rejoiced in December 2000 when the Supreme Court intruded and halted the recount. By a vote of five to four, the nation's highest court overruled the Florida court and gave Florida's electoral vote to Bush, thus deciding the national election—271 electoral votes for Bush and 266 for Gore. Dissenting Justice Steven Breyer warned that "by embroiling our-

selves in a political maelstrom" the Supreme Court risked a "self-inflicted wound . . . that may harm not just the court, but the nation."

The Best Oligarchy Money Can Buy

Whatever else, George W. had a golden touch. Dubya's number-

The Miami Herald
MORIN 12/14/00

one career patron, the Enron Corporation, delivered $550,025 to his two gubernatorial runs and his 2000 presidential campaign. With more than $1.8 million in contributions, Bush got more money from the energy industry during 1999–2000 than any other federal candidate in the previous decade. Houston-based Enron donated $2.3 million to Republicans in the 1999–2000 elections—about $1 million more than number-two-ranked Exxon-Mobil.

The Miami Herald

Did patrons get what they paid for? In their first one hundred days, and during the next eight years, President Bush and Vice President Cheney, both former oil executives, backed their friends in the energy businesses with repeated calls to allow drilling in the Arctic National Wildlife Refuge and on other federal lands. Bush and Cheney then tried to keep the federal government from intervening in the California energy crisis, which helped Enron and other energy wholesalers rack up record profits. Bush sided with the coal mining and electricity industries when he reversed a campaign pledge to reduce carbon dioxide emissions and announced the U.S. rejection of the Kyoto Protocol.

The character and likely outcomes of the Bush administration were clear within a few years, but nearly half the electorate voted for Bush again in 2004. To be sure, a disputed election in one state—this time, Ohio—threw the majority of electoral votes to Bush. In Ohio, as in Florida four years before, the Republican secretary of state, J. Kenneth Blackwell, was at once the state's top

The Campaign Contributors...

The Miami Herald
MARin

ing machines that left no paper trail and were sold by Diebold, whose CEO Walden O'Dell was a Republican fund-raiser. One Bush "pioneer" fund-raiser in Ohio, Tom Noe, got a twenty-seven-month federal sentence in 2006 for illegally laundering more than $45,000 to the Bush-Cheney ticket in 2004, plus another eighteen years for theft, corruption, and forgery. "By their friends you shall know them."

More than a century earlier, Mark Twain gave a formula for interpreting election talk: "It was very simple: you discounted a statement 97 percent; the rest was fact." He noted that the "gilded minority" ruling some countries chose to march at the head of the procession, its banners flying. It "elected itself to be the Nation." This gilded minority

election official *and* state chairman of the Bush election campaign. Like Harris, Blackwell managed to keep voters in Democratic precincts waiting in long lines, denied many of them ballots on procedural technicalities, and arranged things so many votes were never counted. Blackwell opted for touch-screen vot-

21

came to believe the "innumerable claims permitted it for so long that they came to accept [them] as a truth; and not only that, but to believe it right and as it should be." (*A Connecticut Yankee in King Arthur's Court* [1889], chapter 13.)

CHAPTER
3
The Politics of Wealth

"Our prosperity depends on free trade, less regulation, and America's strong place in our global economy. More than ever, American jobs depend on America's standing in the world."

—George W. Bush
at the swearing-in ceremony for
Paul H. O'Neill as secretary of the
treasury, January 30, 2001

WHAT HAPPENED to the confidence felt by most Americans in 2000 about their economic futures? For more than a century the United States has produced more goods and services than any other country—at least one-fifth of the world's total. Under President Ronald Reagan and then under George W. Bush, however, the United States also became the world's largest debtor. By 2008 the United States' gross domestic product approached $15 *trillion*, but the national debt was nearing $10 trillion. Just the interest on the debt amounted to $1.5 billion every day. As the nation aged, bills for Social Security and Medicare would mount. Some analysts expected future deficits to exceed $50 trillion.

The Clinton administration reversed the debt and spending trends set in the Reagan years. For the first time in four decades, the federal budget in the late 1990s achieved a substantial surplus: George W. inherited an economy in which federal revenues had reached nearly 21 percent of GDP, while spending had fallen to below 19 percent. Had these trends continued under President Bush, the U.S. Treasury would have enjoyed a $6 trillion surplus.

From Surplus to Deficit

The Bush team promptly ambushed both the Democratic success story and the conservative ideals of a balanced budget and a limited government. Under the Bush administration, the ratio of spending to revenues reversed. The federal government consumed ever more of the gross domestic product—rising to 20 percent by 2005, while federal revenues shrank to 16 or 17 percent of GDP. In 2008, there were government outlays of $3.1 trillion dollars—up from less than $1.9 trillion in the 2001 budget that Bush inherited from Clinton. Much of the increase came from increases in military spending—up by 30 percent from 2001 to 2008. But subsidies to big farmers also rose during the first seven years of the Bush presidency, even as small farmers went bankrupt.

The Bush administration expanded the federal debt in two ways. First, it cut taxes—mainly for the rich—so that government revenues decreased in 2001–2002 and then could not keep up with mounting outlays for the Iraq war and other defense spending. The war in Iraq also expanded the government payrolls as Washington hired more private contractors and mercenaries to do jobs that might have been done by civil servants and soldiers.

Privatization of this kind made "government" and U.S. armed forces look smaller than they really were, but private contractors were far more expensive and difficult to control than uniformed troops and civil servants. One leading contractor was the Halliburton Company, which was led by Dick Cheney before he became vice president. Halliburton and its Kellogg, Brown & Root

MORiN 05/16/02
The Miami Herald

subsidiary "won" noncompetitive contracts in 2002–2003 to restore Iraq's oil infrastructure, truck in fuel oil from Jordan, build barracks for U.S. troops, and feed them. Starting from zero in early 2003, Halliburton's revenues for work in Iraq rose to $16 billion in the first three years after the U.S. invasion. Halliburton's stock rose four-fold in those three years—an increase that followed the same upward slant as U.S. deaths—from zero toward four thousand.

Money and Political Bedfellows

The Bush administration's penchant for favoritism and special interests reinforced that of an alliance of lobbyists and Republican legislators known as "the K Street Project," which developed after the 1994 elections gave a majority of seats to Republican candidates. Republican Congressman Tom DeLay and his K Street Project helped to make Jack Abramoff the king of GOP lobbyists. The attitude of the new majority—"to the victors go the spoils"—meshed perfectly with Abramoff's style. He promised clients a direct link to the most powerful leaders in Congress and, subsequently, to the Bush White House.

After a decade of big money

Why did the CONgressmen cross the ROAD?...

MORIN
The Miami Herald

and high living, Abramoff's deeds caught up with him. He was convicted in early 2006 of three criminal felony counts. Investigations into Abramoff's network also led to the conviction of White House officials J. Steven Griles and David Safavian, U.S. Representative Bob Ney, and nine other lobbyists and Congressional aides, several of whom had worked for DeLay. The House Government

Reform Committee reported in September 2006 that Abramoff's billing records showed 485 contacts between Abramoff and his lobbyist team and key White House officials, including at least ten direct contacts between Abramoff and Karl Rove.

Delay was indicted in September 2005 by a grand jury in Texas for criminal violation of state election laws. On October 19, 2005, a Texas court issued a warrant for his arrest. Unfazed by all this, President Bush said in December 2005 that he thought DeLay was innocent and hoped DeLay could return to the post of House majority leader.

In the same interview in which the president expressed confidence in Delay's innocence, Bush

also had praise for Rove, his deputy chief of staff and senior adviser, who was being investigated in the CIA leak case involving Valerie Plame Wilson.

Special Interests and the Budget Deficit

The president's 2008 State of the Union address complained that the Democratic Congress had padded the current budget with nearly twelve thousand earmarks to benefit special interests at a cost of $17 billion. But Bush's 2009 budget proposal not only retained but expanded many earmarks. When Republicans dominated Congress in 2005, there were even more pork barrel projects—nearly fourteen thousand costing $27.3 billion. In the late 1990s Congress had funded fewer than three thousand such projects.

The U.S. federal budget deficit was expected to reach 3.4 percent of GDP in 2008.

After the U.S. economy lost seventeen thousand jobs in January 2008, the president in February signed a two-year, $170 billion economic stimulus package— what he called "a booster shot" to

an ailing American economy. Tax rebate checks worth more than 1 percent of GDP would go to 128 million families. Thanks to last-minute pressures from Democrats, the package included

checks for 20 million low-income seniors, who were quite likely to spend the money promptly. But the stimulus package did nothing to expand unemployment insurance or invest in roads, bridges,

the
BUSH SOCIAL
SECURITY
SAFETY NET...

MORÍN
8/13/05
The Miami Herald

schools, or water systems—moves that would have garnered more bang for the buck and helped financially strapped states. When the stock market continued to roil in March 2008, the federal government offered $200 billion to financial institutions to encourage them to start loaning money again—another hoped-for quick-fix for deep problems.

Making Big Government Bigger

At the same time, Bush ambushed the Republican Party's asserted preference for smaller government. The total number of federal employees held steady at just over 3 million from 2002 to 2005. This total included nearly 2 million civil servants and 1.4 million military personnel, plus fewer than 1 million postal workers. But there was also a hidden work force of nearly *11 million* by 2005—those paid from government grants (nearly 3 million) or working on contracts (almost 8 million in 2005—up from 5 million in 2002).

Bottom of Form

A staunch supporter of Reaganomics, Bruce Bartlett concluded that George W. Bush was an "impostor"—neither a Reagan nor even a Nixon. He contended that Bush's tax cuts and trade policies bankrupted America and would cost future taxpayers dearly. Former Federal Reserve chairman Alan Greenspan reached similar conclusions.

When Paul O'Neil, Bush's first secretary of the treasury, warned that huge tax increases would be needed to forestall national bankruptcy, he was forced to resign.

Binge Consumption

Besides the federal budget deficit, the U.S. economy also suffered from a widening trade gap. The

spread between U.S. imports and exports reached $63 billion in 2007. Much of this deficit, as well as U.S. budget shortfalls, was bankrolled by China and Japan.

Was it wise for Americans to let foreigners finance their binges? Both China and Japan wanted to prop up the dollar so that their own goods would be cheap for U.S. buyers. But their willingness to accept American debt wavered as the dollar entered a free fall next to the euro. China and Japan began to shift

some of their surplus funds to Europe. As this process gathered momentum, the dollar sank still further. The fall of the dollar led some economists to call for a return to the gold standard.

Regressive Tax Cuts Redux

From 2001 to 2008 the number-one domestic priority for the Bush team was lower taxes for the rich. According to the Reaganomics doctrine espoused by Bushites, more money in the pocket of rich Americans would lead them to increase investments in businesses that would then generate employment for everyone else. The theory had been tested and shown false in the 1980s, but it appealed to George W. and many of his corporate

supporters. Thanks to several waves of tax cuts, from 2001 through 2008, the rich became much richer, but real incomes for most Americans stayed flat or declined.

Job creation was weak under the Bush presidency and demand for services and hard goods anemic. As a result, rich Americans had poor incentives to invest in job-creating businesses. Far from

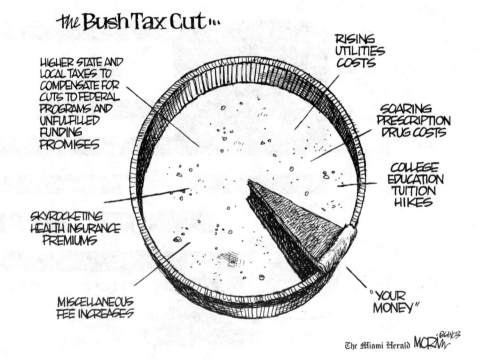

the Bush Tax Cut ...

HIGHER STATE AND LOCAL TAXES TO COMPENSATE FOR CUTS TO FEDERAL PROGRAMS AND UNFULFILLED FUNDING PROMISES

RISING UTILITIES COSTS

SOARING PRESCRIPTION DRUG COSTS

COLLEGE EDUCATION TUITION HIKES

SKYROCKETING HEALTH INSURANCE PREMIUMS

"YOUR MONEY"

MISCELLANEOUS FEE INCREASES

The Miami Herald MORIN 8/61/03

employing more Americans, many U.S. corporations terminated jobs for U.S. workers and hired workers abroad at cut-rate prices. Many economists who had extolled free trade as a virtual panacea for material well-being changed their tune. The loss of technology as well as jobs from outsourcing was creating problems not compensated by cheap goods in Wal-Mart. Unsafe toys and food from countries with lax standards were no bargain, whatever the price.

The Miami Herald

The U.S. economy grew an average of 3.8 percent in Clinton's two terms. It averaged just 2.4 percent under President Bush in 2001–2007. Less growth meant fewer jobs and lower incomes for many Americans. During the Bush years the gap between America's richest and poorest grew to its widest in at least twenty-five years. Data released by the Internal Revenue Service showed that the richest 1 percent of Americans received 21.2 percent of all U.S. income in 2005. Meanwhile, 95 percent of Americans reported smaller incomes in 2005 than in 2000.

Me First

The author of *Das Kapital* oversimplified, but the greedy behavior of many in the Bush administration would make Karl Marx cheer and proclaim: "I was right: Economics determines politics, law, and culture. Ideology is nothing but a mask for material self-interest. Those who control the means of production are the real rulers. They pull the strings of political puppets who serve their narrow interests. The ruling class does not need troops to enforce the status quo. Why use violence when brainwashing can do the same job? The goals of the economic elite are served by the entire edifice of religion, education, and communications. Many who profit from the existing system believe that they have every right to do so. Some think that, since they prosper, God must be on their side: They deserve tax cuts and subsidies."

Results of Bushonomics

As the Bush presidency whimpered to an end in 2008, the results of Bushonomics were tragically clear. Profligate spending plus tax cuts fostered an all-around malaise that tipped the economy into recession.

The share of Americans living in poverty shot up from 11.3 percent in 2000 to 12.3 percent in 2006—a total of 36.5 million. Thirteen million families experienced what the U.S. Census Bureau called low or very low "food security." Nearly a quarter of all blacks lived in poverty, a fifth of all Hispanics, one-tenth of Asians, and 8.2 percent of whites. Almost a tenth of people age sixty-five and older spent their declining years in poverty.

The tax cuts that left some peo-

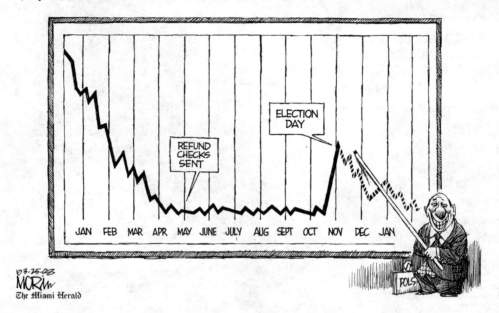

HOW the ECONOMIC STIMULUS PACKAGE WORKS

ELECTION DAY

REFUND CHECKS SENT

JAN FEB MAR APR MAY JUNE JULY AUG SEPT OCT NOV DEC JAN

03-15-03
MORIN
The Miami Herald

POLS

ple with more money in their pockets were financed with government borrowing. "Debt is future taxes," the Cato Institute warned. "Deficit spending on the [Iraq] war and other items will make taxpayers worse off in the future."

America's balance sheet turned negative. While other economies surged, the United States slowed and then slipped back. The tallest building, the largest mall, the highest Ferris wheel took shape elsewhere. So did the top scores in science and math. America's

coffers were emptying, even as the share of Americans living in poverty increased.

Faith, Education, & Science

"Our priorities is our faith."

—George W. Bush
in Greensboro, North Carolina,
October 10, 2000

PRESIDENTIAL CANDIDATE George W. Bush told Americans that he would not impose his religious beliefs on others. The future president said that he had stopped boozing and turned to Jesus in 1985 after meeting with the Reverend Billy Graham. On his first day in the White House in 2001, however, the reborn Christian proclaimed January 21 a day of prayer and thanksgiving.

For the next eight years, the president's faith shaped his policies in ways that challenged the First Amendment's separation of church and state. Bush persuaded Congress to fund the social welfare activities of "faith-based" institutions. He blocked legislation to fund stem-cell research. He aligned himself with those who opposed same-sex unions, abortion, contraceptives, and sex education. He sought to appoint judges who would back his "values" agenda.

Faith-Based Initiatives

Bush established a White House Office of Faith-Based and Community Initiatives in January 2001. The very first program he sent to Congress was an educa-

tional reform package that included vouchers for private schools—what he called "opportunity scholarships." Religious conservatives took heart when in June 2002 the U.S. Supreme Court ruled five to four that school vouchers did not violate the constitutional mandate to keep church separate from state.

Critics complained that vouchers diverted funds from public education, that public subsidies to parochial schools violated the First Amendment, and that reliance on government money invited government regulation of religion.

The first director of the Office of Faith-Based Initiatives, John DiIulio, had a different complaint. He resigned in August 2001, charging that the president had forsaken compassionate conser-

YOU'RE POOR? TOUGH LUCK.

SEX DISCRIMINATION VICTIM? DON'T BREAK MY HEART!

CAMPAIGN FAIRNESS? MONEY TALKS!

CORPORATE POWER RULES!

STUDENT FREE SPEECH? SHUT UP.

SCHOOL INTEGRATION? HOW RACIST!!

CONGRESS? OVERRULED!!

AFFIRMATIVE ACTION? STOP YOUR WHINING!

ABORTION PRECEDENT? DROP DEAD.

OH, YEAH...
... AND NO JUDICIAL ACTIVISM!

07.11.07
MORIN
The Miami Herald

The Miami Herald
MORIN

that were, in reality, designed to mobilize "religious voters in 20 targeted races."

Faith-Based Education: "Intelligent Design"

Long after the Scopes trial of 1925, the U.S. Supreme Court, in 1987, finally struck down all state laws requiring that "creationism" be taught in any public school where evolution was discussed. President Bush, however, sided with those Americans and state boards of education, as in Kansas, demanding that creationism be taught in public schools along with evolution. Most scientists saw advocacy of intelligent design—a.k.a. creationism—as another step in dumbing down Americans. Intelligent design is

vatism for tax cuts. Similar complaints were registered by David Kuo after he resigned as deputy director of the Office of Faith-Based Initiatives. Kuo told the press in October 2006 that the office was mainly used to mount ostensibly nonpartisan events

not a tested scientific theory, they said, but a cleverly marketed strategy to indoctrinate students into Christian conservative ideology.

No Child Left Behind?

American students scored lower in math and reading than their peers in most industrialized coun-tries. The United Nations in 2003 reported that nearly one-fifth of the U.S. population was function-ally illiterate. The president's No Child Left Behind Act aimed to make all children proficient in reading and mathematics by 2014. The act promised federal aid to achieve these goals, but the presi-dent never requested, and Con-gress never provided, funding at the levels Bush pledged. NCLB started from a dubious premise. It assumed, in Bush's phrase, that "measuring is the gateway to suc-cess." Promising "accountability," NCLB depended on high-stakes tests to measure progress. But standardized testing pushes teachers to "teach to the test" rather than to foster creativity and enthusiasm for learning. The emphasis on testing discourages some weaker students and

prompts many to drop out. It encourages administrators to falsify results. Finally, NCLB contributed to what some critics called a "proficiency illusion" because the law allowed each state to define "proficiency." Thus, reading and math tests in Texas and Ohio were *much* easier than in California and Massachusetts. The law tempted states to "define proficiency downward."

Faith-Based Science

The president's values also led him to block several branches of science. Speaking from his Crawford, Texas, ranch on August 9, 2001, the president told Americans: "I strongly oppose human cloning. . . . We recoil at the idea of growing human beings for spare body parts, or creating life for our convenience." He ordered that all federal funding of stem cell research be limited to a handful of preexisting "lines" of cells that had been created specifically for research. He said it would be wrong to use tax dollars to pay for the destruction of more embryos. As he spoke, of course,

THE PRO-LIFE PARTY...

18,000 AMERICANS DIE EACH YEAR DUE TO LACK OF HEALTH INSURANCE ...

THE RIGHT TO BEAR ARMS

GUN DEATHS RISING IN U.S. ...

TRY ABSTINENCE!

AIDS DEATHS IN 2005: APPROX. 3 MILLION

INCREASED ENVIRONMENTAL POLLUTION LINKED TO U.S. URBAN DEATH RATES ...

CIVILIAN WAR DEAD IN IRAQ, LEBANON, AND AFGHANISTAN ...

SAVE the STEM CELLS!!

LIFE

45

thousands of embryos were being destroyed in fertility clinics—created in petri dishes and then discarded. Given the president's logic, he should have shut down every fertility clinic.

Sophistry in High Places

The president and his cronies did not provide inspiring role models for aspiring learners. The president read little and mangled the language.

Worse, he was no curious George. He went by instinct and showed little interest in facts that might contravene his assumptions. His brainier advisers were more adept at sophistry and spin than in the pursuit of knowledge. The editors of *Scientific American* charged in May 2004 that the

MORIN ©9/4/00 The Miami Herald

Bush administration relied on ideological bias instead of science to guide policy.

Bush's disdain for science did not change over the course of his two administrations. On February 14, 2008, the Union of Concerned Scientists issued a report entitled "Federal Science and the Public Good." It called on the next president and Congress to end political interference in science and establish conditions that would allow federal science to flourish. The 2008 statement was signed by Nobel laureates and scientists with significant federal government experience—a former National Science Foundation director, a former presidential science adviser, and a former director of the National Institutes of Health.

Budgeting for Education and Science

The Bush administration complacently cut funding for education and science in its fiscal year 2009 budget. True to its ideology, the Bush administration left the main burdens for education to individuals and local and state governments. The Achilles Heel of this approach was that many individuals and communities are poor. A federal government able to draw on all the revenues and credit of an economic superpower could finance a long war, support big agriculture, and fund many benefits for retirees. But it gave mostly lip service to the educational needs of poor- and middle-income Americans. It generously funded research for advanced weapons and for carbon-based energy, but it shortchanged basic science and alternative energy research.

The Bush fiscal year 2009 budget essentially froze funding for the Department of Education at $59 billion—about the cost of six months' fighting in Iraq. The budget offered a trivial increase for NCLB to a total of $25 billion. It provided only a 3 percent increase for Title I to help low-income children—a projected total of $14 million. The FY 2009 budget cut Teacher Quality State Grants by $100 million. The budget would cover only 17 percent of the nation's costs for special education—less than half the amount promised by Congress some thirty-three years earlier. As if to rub it in, Bush's budget would cut Medicaid-based reimbursements for special education students by $3.6 billion over the next five years. The president's budget included yet another voucher scheme—this time proposing to redirect $300 million into a private school voucher program called "Pell Grants for Kids."

Meanwhile, the average cost of attending a public college rose from $10,000 in 2000 to $13,000 in

2006. But the Bush budget for FY 2009 cut support for low- and middle-income students who were hoping to attend college.

Instead of helping minority education, the budget totally eliminated funding for tribal colleges and universities, Alaska Native/Native Hawaiian institutions, and slashed support for both historically black colleges and universities and Hispanic-serving institutions. The president drew loud applause during his 2008 State of the Union address when he called on Congress to allow U.S. troops to transfer their unused education benefits to family members. One week later, however, when Bush submitted his $3.1 trillion federal budget to Congress, he included no funding for such an initiative.

Finally, the "education president" continued his eight-year

The Miami Herald

trend of shortchanging America's youngest children by failing to expand early learning opportunities for infants, toddlers, and preschoolers with disabilities; failing to fund a program that supports early childhood teacher quality; cutting child care funding for an additional one hundred thousand families; and undermining Head Start by inadequate funding.

Social Costs

"Education" comes from the Latin for "lead out" or "bring up." But American education falls short on both goals. Not only do American pupils do poorly in math and language compared with those in other industrialized countries, but many wind up in jail.

A huge segment of the U.S. population is behind bars—one in a hundred adults was in prison in 2007 (a higher rate than in any other country—about nine times

the rate in Germany, for example). The rate for Hispanic men was one in thirty-six; for adult black males, one in fifteen; for black males aged twenty to thirty-four, a mind-numbing one in nine. The average cost for imprisoning one person per year is $24,000—nearly twice the tuition at a public college. The rising burden on state budgets is severe. On average, states spend 7 percent of their budgets on corrections. Adjusted for inflation, prison costs increased by 127 percent in the twenty years 1987–2007. Opportunity costs were incalculable. What if, instead of serving time, those behind bars were working and playing a constructive role in family and social life? What if, instead of locking up criminals (including marijuana users), the country spent comparable resources on preschool, school, and afterschool activities to "lead out" and "bring up" its young people? What if, instead of fostering conditions where young people spend half their time doing minimum-wage jobs, we helped them to devote full time to developing their minds and bodies? Would this not be a real contribution to "values"?

Health of the Nation

*"I mean, people have access
to health care in America.
After all, you just go to an
emergency room."*

—George W. Bush
    July 10, 2007, Cleveland, Ohio

SOMETHING IS WRONG. Americans spend more than any other Western country or Japan on medical treatment but, on average, die earlier. Despite America's great wealth and leading role in medical research, many poor people do not go for treatment except to hospital emergency rooms. Many elderly people fret whether they can pay for the prescribed drugs they need. Some treatment for veterans is world class but much is a soul-wrenching scandal. Gun deaths mount. Something is broken and getting worse.

The Miami Herald

Babies Dying, Mothers Too

The single best indicator of social malaise is infant mortality—a reflection of poverty, poor education, and a lack of medical services. Twice as many babies die in their first year in the United States as in Japan. The United Nations, in 2006, reported that average infant mortality in the United States was 6.3 for 1,000 live births—slightly better than Croatia's 6.4, but much worse than Cuba's 5.1 rate, and not even close to Iceland's 2.9 rate. In parts of the United States, things got worse under George W. Bush. The number of babies dying in Washington, DC, *increased* from 10.5 per 1,000 in 2003 to 12 per 1,000 in 2004. The number in Louisiana rose from 9.3 in 2003 to 11.4 in 2005. Rates in Alabama, Tennessee, Louisiana, and the Carolinas also increased in these years. Meanwhile, maternal mortality in the United States—11 deaths per 100,000 live births—was double the rate in most other industrialized countries.

The Uninsured Society

Americans paid out more for health care in the Bush years but got no more in return. In 2000,

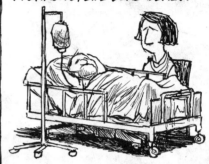

total U.S. outlays for medical care amounted to $1.345 trillion. Total expenditures in 2006 reached $2.122 trillion. More than half came from private sources ($251 billion out of pocket and $727 billion by insurance) and $997 billion from government (three-fourths from Washington; one-fourth from states).

The United States is the only major industrialized country without universal health care. Some 64 percent of Americans received employment-based health insur-

ance in 2000, but that percentage declined to 59.7 by 2006. The annual cost of family health insurance premiums in 2000 (adjusted for inflation) was $7,643. In 2006 that cost rose to $11,480. Nearly 11 percent of white Americans had no insurance; the percentage of uninsured blacks and Hispanics was much higher.

The number of Americans without health insurance increased from 38.4 million in 2000 to 46.9 million in 2006. Though that total included 8.7 million children, President Bush twice blocked additional health insurance for children.

Poverty and Health

Driven by ideology and beholden to private insurance firms, the Bush administration delivered a double whammy to public health: It permitted the number of uninsured Americans to increase and fostered greater income inequality. Poverty, in turn, conduced to unhealthy lifestyles—poor nutrition, limited access to medical care, physical insecurity. From 2003 to 2004 the percentage of Americans under eighteen living in poverty rose from 16.3 percent to 17.6 percent. Poverty correlated with single moms struggling to shield offspring from street violence, drug addiction, and jail.

Income gaps go far to explain health gaps. The United States has the most income inequality of any Westernized economy—twice the rate in Japan and a quarter more than Canada. Many more people in the United States live in poverty than in other Westernized countries.

Veterans

President Bush called it a sacred duty to care for the veterans who have defended America. If so, the duty has been badly botched. To be sure, far more of those wounded in Afghanistan or Iraq survive than in previous wars, but many of the survivors are amputees or brain injured; at least one-quarter have psychological wounds. Treatment for such persons, even at the premier military hospital, Walter Reed Medical Center, became a national scandal in 2007.

As in other arenas, the White House punished whistleblowers such as Congressman Christo-

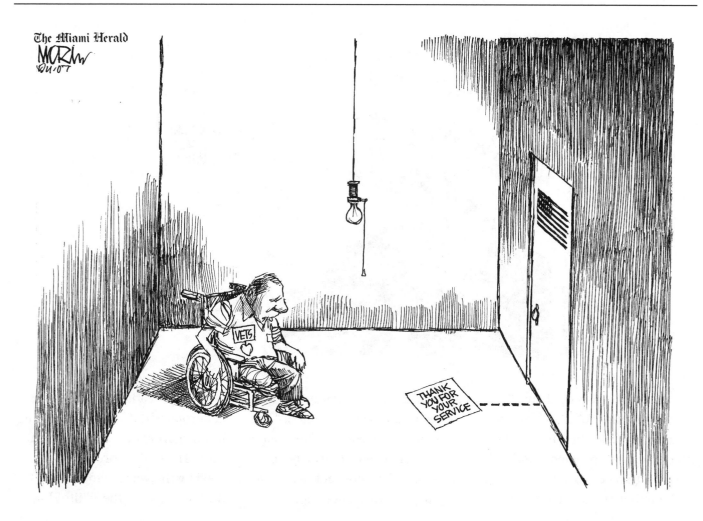

pher H. Smith (R-NJ), chair of the House Veterans Affairs Committee during Bush's first term, who tried to expose problems and improve things. When he was sacked, Richard B. Fuller, a

spokesman for the Paralyzed Veterans of America, explained: "The Republicans needed a chairman who would consistently say no to veterans' groups and say yes to the Republican leadership."

The Bush administration was generous with funds to fight wars but niggardly in caring for its victims. The budget proposed in 2005 by the war aficionado–draft dodgers in the White House

The Miami Herald
MORIN 8/12/03

YOU'LL LIKE IT...
TRUST US!!

INSURANCE INDUSTRY

DRUG INDUSTRY

CON GRESS

The MEDICARE BILL VOL. 1

called for an increase in drug co-pays by veterans from $7 to $15 for a thirty-day supply. The White House called for eliminating a $100 million program of grants to states for extended care of veter-

ans in state-sponsored nursing homes. The government billed veterans for missing helmets un-less they could prove the loss happened as they were wounded.

Privatization also played a role.

Reports that Walter Reed would be privatized harmed morale and efficiency. In 2006 the army awarded the five-year, $120 mil-lion contract to IAP World Ser-vices, managed by two former

3,000 PEOPLE DIE IN TERRORIST ATTACK AGAINST U.S. ON 9-11 ""

The Miami Herald

18,000 PEOPLE DIE PREMATURELY EACH YEAR IN U.S. DUE TO LACK OF AFFORDABLE HEALTH INSURANCE ""

"" WE CAN'T AFFORD IT!

employees of Kellogg, Brown & Root (KBR), the notorious Halliburton subsidiary. IAP, where former Vice President Dan Quayle is a director, showed its mettle in 2005 when it bungled delivery of ice to victims of Hurricane Katrina. Still, its volume of business with Uncle Sam grew from $222 million in 2000 to $1.2 billion in 2005.

Will Things Get Better in Fiscal Year 2009?

President Bush's $3 trillion budget for 2009 aspired to balance the budget by 2012. One tool would be to limit federal health care entitlements. The growth of such programs would be trimmed by $208 billion over five years. Most of the cuts would come

from Medicare—largely from freezing payments to doctors, hospitals, and other care providers. Nursing homes and teaching hospitals, which provide free service for indigents, would also

be hurt. Washington gave out "stimulus" refunds in 2008, even as it sought to cut jobs for nurses and other medical personnel.

A related issue is retirement income. In 2005 President Bush

proposed the creation of "personal" Social Security savings accounts to give workers more control over their money and get a higher rate of return than funds held by the government. Wall Street cheered, but most Republicans as well as Democrats thought this a nonstarter. Private accounts would not ensure the long-term solvency of Social Security. Nor was it likely that most workers would maintain private accounts or invest prudently. Bush's idea of privatizing retirement experienced a timely death in 2007.

A World Leader

A health problem the United States does not share with other rich nations is deaths by firearms. The United States has by far the highest rate of gun deaths—murders, suicides, and accidents—among the world's thirty-six richest nations. Gun-related deaths in the United States have been five to six times higher than in Europe or Australia and ninety-five times higher than in Asia. Japan had the lowest rate, followed by Asia's "Little Tigers"—South Korea, Hong Kong, Singapore, and Tai-

wan. But low rates were not due to Confucian ethics or race. England's rate was just above Taiwan's.

Some thirty-one thousand Americans were killed by firearms in 2005—up from 28,663 in 2000. Half those killed were suicides, mostly by older people, but deaths among young people were high as well. One white male aged seventeen or younger was killed every thirty hours; one young black male, every twenty-four hours. Girls were not exempt: One female seventeen or younger was shot and killed every two days.

"If you have a country saturated with guns—available to people when they are intoxicated, angry, or depressed—it's not unusual guns will be used more often," said Rebecca Peters, a Johns Hopkins University fellow spe-

cializing in gun violence. "This has to be treated as a public health emergency."

The National Rifle Association countered that gun death statistics confused cause and effect.

The NRA urged U.S. lawmakers to stand by the Second Amendment protection of the right to "keep and bear arms." The organization's top command assured members in 2000 that, with Bush as president, the NRA would operate from inside the Oval Office. It expected also that the Supreme Court would "back us to the hilt."

The NRA and other gun rights groups gave at least $20 million to federal candidates and party committees from 1990 through 2006—most of it to Republicans. Their donations exceeded those of gun control advocates by ten to one. The gun lobby's donations reached $4 million in the 2000 elections.

NRA membership stands at about 3.8 million in 2008, down about two hundred thousand from 2004. But the relatively small rank and file can have outsized political impact because their members vote at a higher rate—95 percent—than the overall electorate. The NRA also invests millions in campaign tele-

The Miami Herald

vision and billboard advertising. Delivery of its 15 million-strong direct-mail voter scorecard can move the polls in House races overnight. Richard Feldman, a

former gun lobbyist and NRA insider called the NRA a "cynical, mercenary political cult."

As governor of Texas, George W. Bush signed a law allowing

SILENCER...

GUN MAKER. DEALER
LAWSUIT PROTECTION

GUN

DEATHS

CON
GRESS

04/25/03
MORIN
The Miami Herald

ten years. Bush also helped block House attempts to close the "gun show loophole" allowing unlicensed dealers to sell weapons without requesting a government background check.

Vice President Cheney, for his part, took an even stronger stand against gun control. Having shot his own hunting companion two years earlier, the Veep, on February 9, 2008, joined 55 Senators and 250 House members in asking the Supreme Court to uphold a ruling by the U.S. Court of Appeals for the DC Circuit that the District of Columbia's ban on handguns is unconstitutional. The NRA called the congressional brief "a historical message to the court" that Congress believes the Second Amendment guarantees an individual right to possess firearms. The NRA said it was

people to carry concealed weapons. In 2004, he joined the NRA in pressuring Congress to make gun dealers as well as manufacturers immune to civil lawsuits. He helped persuade the Senate to reject a House effort to extend the existing ban on the manufacture and import of certain military assault weapons for

A WELL-REGULATED MILITIA BEING NECESSARY TO THE SECURITY OF A FREE STATE, THE RIGHT OF THE PEOPLE TO KEEP AND BEAR ARMS SHALL NOT BE INFRINGED.

SCHOOL

The Miami Herald

"grateful and fortunate to have a friend of freedom in the vice president." Vice President Cheney deviated from the stand taken by the U.S. Solicitor General Paul D. Clement. The solicitor agreed that the Supreme Court should recognize the individual right but said the lower court's ruling was so broad it could endanger federal gun control measures such as a ban on possession of new machine guns. White House spokesman Tony Fratto explained President Bush's position: "Like the members of Congress who signed the amicus brief, the president strongly believes that the Consti-

tution protects an individual right to keep and bear firearms," but "leaves procedural questions to the lawyers."

A spate of shootings around the country in late 2007–early 2008 did not pry the White House and Congress from the embrace of the NRA. But the District of Columbia ban on handguns harmonized with the position adopted by most of the nation's appeals courts: The Second Amendment guarantees a right to bear arms only as a *collective, civic right related to military service.* This interpretation was confirmed by a unanimous opinion of the Supreme Court (*United States v. Miller*) in 1939.

Upending nearly seventy years of precedent, the Supreme Court in June 2008 struck down the District of Columbia's ban on handgun possession and decided for the first time in U.S. history that the Second Amendment guarantees an individual's right to own a gun for self-defense. The Court's landmark five-to-four decision wiped away years of lower court decisions holding that the intent of the Second Amendment was to tie the right of gun possession to militia service. Justice Antonin Scalia wrote for the majority: "We hold that the District's ban on handgun possession in the home violates the Second Amendment, as does its prohibition against ren-

dering any lawful firearm in the home operable for the purpose of immediate self-defense."

President Bush approved: "As a long-standing advocate of the rights of gun owners in America, I applaud the Supreme Court's historic decision today confirming [that] the Second Amendment protects an individual right to keep and bear firearms." Senator John McCain called the decision a "landmark victory" for Second Amendment rights. Seeking the best of both worlds, Senator Barack Obama said he had "always believed that the Second Amendment protects the right of individuals to bear arms," but that he also identified "with the need for crime-ravaged communities to save their children from the violence that plagues our streets

through commonsense, effective safety measures."

Arlene Goldsmith, Executive Director of New Alternatives for Children, invited the Supreme Court majority to meet "some children who have been victims of random shootings in their own neighborhoods, like the child we serve with a bullet lodged in his lung that cannot be removed."

Just before the Court's decision was announced, a worker in a Kentucky plastics plant shot his supervisor, four coworkers, and himself to death.

Gun deaths are a small part of the nation's health problem, but they contributed to a larger syndrome in which aggressive individualism often prevailed over cooperative problem-solving.

Energy & the Environment

"Conservation may be a sign of personal virtue, but it is not a sufficient basis for a sound comprehensive energy policy."

—Dick Cheney
to the Associated Press,
April 30, 2001

THE TWO FORMER OILMEN elected or nearly elected to boss the United States in 2000 and 2004 pledged to make the country "energy independent." The president also promised clean skies and green forests. But nearly all the administration's actions gave the lie to both promises. The evidence suggested that the president and vice president were in thrall to the oil, gas, and coal magnates who funded their election campaigns and to the House of Saud, long a partner with the Bush dynasty. From 2001 through 2008, the profits of oil conglomerates such as Exxon and carbon exporters such as Saudi Arabia and Russia went through the roof. The United

States became not less but more dependent on external suppliers. Americans imported 30 percent of their energy in 2007. Meanwhile, the more fossil fuels burned by Americans and others, the more the globe suffered from pollution and overheating. Conservation, said Dick Cheney, is a private virtue. Burning carbons, he might have added, produces losses for public welfare but nets billions and even trillions for purveyors of fossil fuels.

The man from whom Bush took the presidency in 2000, Al Gore, won a Nobel Peace Prize for alerting millions to the dangers of global warming. But the message of Gore's film, *An Inconvenient Truth*, did little to shake Bush's policies on energy and the environment.

America has been a danger to

itself and a bad neighbor to the world. With less than 5 percent of the world population, the United States consumes a fourth of the world's resources and produces one-quarter of the emissions that

damage health and the environment. The world's largest economy is wasteful in the extreme. It uses twice the energy employed in Japan or Europe to produce one unit of GDP. It builds roads

and relies heavily on private automobiles with little thought to the social and environmental consequences. It farms intensively using chemical fertilizers and genetic engineering to produce grain-fed beef and chickens but with little effort to conserve land and water. Its power generators belch smoke and fumes that poison communities near and far. Its coal miners blast off mountain tops and let the debris clog the river valleys below. In all of these domains, America sets a model that many other nations, anxious to emulate the good life, follow. In recent years, the chimera of

corn- and sugar-based ethanol did little for the environment but helped double prices on food staples worldwide.

Neither the government nor many Americans seemed to worry much about the toll that daily traffic jams imposed on personal and public health. Automobiles were king. The American model then helped inspire Chinese and Indians to build their own armadas of private automobiles—a certain threat to the entire biosphere.

These baneful practices began long before 2001, but the Bush administration thwarted efforts to

The Miami Herald

change them. Indeed, it revoked earlier restraints and weakened their enforcement. Teddy Roosevelt would not have been pleased.

The Bush mantra for environmental protection was "voluntary restraint." The White House labored to throw off any legal obligation—whether imposed by the U.S. Congress, a state, a multilateral accord, or an international agency—to limit greenhouse gases. The White House muzzled scientists in NASA and other agencies whose research pointed to the impact of human activity on the global climate.

The EPA's efforts under President Bush to weaken environmental protection were so shameless that even Dick Cheney might blush when they were exposed. The Bush administration claimed that it lacked the right to regulate carbon dioxide and other greenhouse gases under the Clean Air Act, and even if it did, it would not use the authority. In April 2007 by a five to four decision, however, the Supreme Court in *Massachusetts et al. v. EPA* ruled that the EPA has the authority to regulate heat-trapping gases in automobile emissions. The court added that the agency cannot sidestep its authority to regulate the gases that

contribute to global climate change unless it can provide a scientific basis for its refusal.

Undaunted in its struggle against environmental protection,

however, the EPA in December 2007, after nearly two years of delay, rejected California's request to regulate tailpipe emissions from passenger cars and light trucks. The EPA argued that state clean car programs of this kind fall outside the scope of the Clean Air Act. The EPA decision had ramifications beyond California and the United States because U.S. cars, though making up just 30 percent of the world's total, account for 45 percent of global automotive carbon dioxide emissions. Arnold Schwarzenegger and thirteen other governors protested.

On February 8, 2008, the U.S. Court of Appeals for the DC Circuit threw out the EPA's approach to limiting mercury emitted from power plant smokestacks, saying the EPA ignored laws and twisted logic when it imposed new standards favorable to plant owners. This court's critique undid a controversial program to "trade" emissions of mercury. The court compared the EPA to the capricious Queen of Hearts in *Alice's Adventures in Wonderland*, saying the agency had followed its own desires and ignored the "plain text" of the law.

Having spurned the Kyoto Protocol in 2001, the Bush administration often cast doubt on climate science. In September 2007, however, President Bush hosted an international climate confer-

ence in Washington. Unlike his earlier performances, Bush now acknowledged risks posed by global warming. Still, he continued to insist on voluntary measures and improved technology as the appropriate solutions. He offered no specific targets or solutions aside from the establishment of an international fund to promote clean energy in the developing world. "It's a fraud," said Stanford climatologist Stephen Schneider. "You can't solve this problem by voluntary measures." Many European countries called for a treaty that would require emissions cuts of more than 50 percent by 2050. Later in the year the U.S. delegation succeeded in sabotaging an international conference in Bali that sought to move beyond Kyoto. The Americans prevented the conference

from agreeing to any specific commitments on reducing greenhouse gases.

The administration's priorities were evident in what it taxed or rewarded. Thus, President Bush's

2007 budget offered paltry support for alternative and renewable energy while providing some $2 billion in tax breaks to the oil and gas industry. Washington turned a blind eye as many firms

The Miami Herald
MORIN ©7/6/00

set up Potemkin offices in off-shore tax havens. In 2007 Halliburton moved its official headquarters to Dubai, even though most management functions remained in Houston. When Cheney was still CEO, Halliburton got a mailbox in the Cayman Islands so it could service Iran's oil industry—otherwise off limits to U.S. firms.

The Bush team supported research in oil, gas, coal, and nuclear energy but gave comparatively little to alternative energy sources. The president requested $25 billion for the U.S. Department of Energy (DoE) in FY 2009. This was not small change but still a trifle next to the $700 to $800 billion requested for defense. Indeed, even the DoE budget devoted nearly *half* of its funds to military activities: more

than $6 billion to improve nuclear weapons, $5.5 billion to clean up "Cold War legacy" waste sites, and $1.8 billion to control nuclear weapons dissemination. By contrast, the DoE Office of Energy Efficiency and Renewable Energy budget would get $1.25 billion, just $1 million more than the previous year. It provided $592 million for ethanol and fuel cell technologies but only $241 million for renewable energy—$225 million for solar, $53 million for wind power, and just $30 million for geothermal.

Though stingy on renewables, the FY 2009 budget was more liberal than its two predecessors, which dropped all funding for hydropower as well as geothermal. Wind power funds decreased by about 4 percent in 2007 and by 9 percent in 2008.

The administration's FY 2009 budget also provided $186 million for energy efficient buildings and industrial technologies. Finally, it included $15 million for the Asia Pacific Partnership to accelerate clean energy globally. It also provided $1.4 billion to promote emissions-free nuclear power, $648 million for clean coal technology, $4.7 billion toward basic science for energy and environmental solutions, and $3.2 billion to advanced nuclear fuel cycle.

Spain and Germany were the leaders in solar energy, but wind power was also being exploited there. Indeed, Europeans had trouble getting all the windmill blades they wanted. Hydro geothermal energy was being harnessed in Iceland, the Philippines, and northern California, but deep down there are huge energy reserves that can be tapped by heat mining. *The Future of Geothermal Energy*, a 2007 study by MIT scientists for the U.S. Department of Energy, concluded that with a reasonable investment in research and development, enhanced geothermal energy could provide 100 GW or more of cost-competitive generating capacity in the next fifty years. The study estimated that commercially viable geothermal energy could be developed in ten to fifteen years. But funding for geothermal energy and for hydropower simply disappeared in the U.S. federal budgets for FY 2007 and 2008.

By its own reckoning, the administration's FY 2009 budget cut nuclear energy research by nearly 11 percent and energy efficiency and renewable energy research programs by nearly 17 percent. According to Dr. Henry Kelly, president of the Federation of American Scientists, the budget gave unwarranted priority to the hugely expensive white elephant called the Global Nuclear Energy Partnership. Kelly said, "Most of the technologies that can actually help meet U.S. energy and climate goals at acceptable prices are cut sharply."

Another problem with reliance on fossil fuels became evident just twenty-four hours after Bush touted clean coal in his January 2008 State of the Union address. The DoE pulled the plug on its FutureGen project to build the first zero-emissions coal plant. In recent days Citigroup and other banks had said they were unlikely to finance more coal-fired plants because their huge carbon footprint provoked opposition across the country.

Instead of pushing to make solar and wind power more cost effective, Bush fought to open federal lands and waters to oil and gas drilling. Instead of protecting the natural reserves, the administration kept Yellowstone National Park open to snowmobiles. It even cut roads into national forests so loggers could fell and haul away some of the oldest and largest trees in the country—at taxpayers' expense.

The administration resisted efforts to raise fuel efficiency standards. Defining sports utility vehicles as trucks, it encouraged Detroit to build and Americans to indulge their passion for gas guzzlers, dangerous to their drivers as well as others on the road. Though Washington subsidized the auto and airplane industries, it balked at helping train and bus systems that could ease congestion and pollution.

The upshot was that the Bush team worked to enrich the producers of fossil fuels regardless of the cost to the environment or family budgets. If hostile regimes in Caracas and Moscow benefited, this was unpleasant but unimportant. The administration also ignored the military and political costs of accessing oil in the Middle East, Azerbaijan, and Kazakhstan. Big oil and military industries, however, were pleased.

"O what a tangled web

we weave,

When first we practise

to deceive!"

—Sir Walter Scott

"We're going to look back at this period of time two decades from now and see a vast expansion of executive authority. And a big part of it is done by the state-secrets doctrine. Do I think in some cases that the government uses it inappropriately? Absolutely."

—Senator Arlen Specter (R-Penn.) quoted by Patrick Radden Keefe, "State Secrets," *The New Yorker*, April 28, 2008, pp. 28–34, quote, p. 31.

GEORGE W. BUSH erected walls around many of his activities before, during, and even after his years in the White House. He sought to expand executive privilege in unprecedented ways—far beyond anything done even by Richard Nixon or Ronald Reagan.

Executive Privilege

On November 1, 2001, Bush issued Executive Order 13233 overriding the 1978 Presidential Records Act. As with his Clean Skies Act, Bush's executive order was named for what it was not—the "Further Implementation of the Presidential Records Act."

The Miami Herald

Rather than "implementing" that statute, the order violated both its spirit and letter. The 1978 act mandated that presidential records should be managed on behalf of the nation by the archivist of the United States and be made available to the public twelve years after the president leaves office. Bush's order gave the White House, as well as *former* presidents, the right to veto the release of such documents, thereby taking the responsibility for administering presidential papers away from the archivist of the United States.

Why did Bush contravene the

1978 statute? The last sentence of the letter announcing his order gave a hint: "This directive again applies also to the vice presidential records of former Vice President George H. W. Bush." Thus, any attempt to link Poppy to the Iran-Contra scandal could be stalled for the indefinite future. Any less than legal actions by the many current holdovers from the Reagan and George H.W. Bush administrations could also be shelved in deep freeze.

The Miami Herald
MORin

Ashcroft and Cheney vs. Freedom of Information

Adding to the movement toward stealth, Attorney General John Ashcroft in fall 2001 told federal agencies (including the National Archives administering the Bush presidential library) that they would be vigorously defended when they withheld records requested under the Freedom of Information Act.

Even more than Bush, Cheney tried to envelop his actions in secrecy. After 9/11, the vice president and a shadow government retreated to undisclosed locations.

Meanwhile, the General Accounting Office (GAO) was seeking to force the White House to disclose information about meetings held by Cheney with industry executives in 2001 before he recommended an energy strategy focused on the opening of environmentally sensitive lands to oil and gas drilling. Cheney, backed by Bush, refused to comply with the GAO request for energy task force records. Hitting a stone wall, the GAO announced in January 2002 that it would take the

White House to court—the first time in the eighty-year history of the investigative arm of Congress that it would sue the executive branch. On December 9, 2002, the U.S. District Court for the District of Columbia dismissed the GAO suit, ruling that Comptroller General David Walker lacked standing. Walker did not appeal.

Secrets of Energy and Politics

The year 2001 also saw the energy wholesaler Enron tank and declare bankruptcy. Enron, too, had thrived on secrecy. It had played an elaborate shell game, hiding debts in some eight hundred offshore tax havens. For years, as political commentator and former Republican party strategist Kevin Phillips put it, the Bush family

and its retainers had clustered around Enron "like bees around a honeycomb." Enron penetrated the Bush team wide and deep. The Veep admitted that, as head

of the Bush administration's energy task force, he had met several times with Enron's Ken Lay.

U.S. Attorney General Ashcroft had to recuse himself from the

Justice Department's Enron investigation because the company had donated nearly $61,000 to his failed 2000 Senate campaign. Bush adviser Rove was a major Enron stockholder when he met Lay to discuss Enron's problems with federal regulators. Bush's first secretary of the army, Thomas White, had worked for Enron for ten years. Former Montana governor Marc Racicot was Enron's chief Washington lobbyist before being named national chairman of the Republican Party. Congressman Tom DeLay danced so well to Enron's tunes that he was known in Austin as "Dereg." U.S. Trade Representative Robert Zoellick had served on Enron's advisory council. Spencer Abraham, Bush's first secretary of energy, took Enron contributions as a senator. At Ken Lay's recommen-

dation, Bush named Patrick H. Wood, III, to chair the Federal Energy Regulatory Commission. Others with close Enron links included White House counsel Alberto Gonzalez, Commerce Secretary Don Evans, and Texas Senator Phil Gramm who, among other exploits, resisted Democratic moves to penalize U.S.

firms using offshore mail drops to avoid U.S. taxes.

Even after the Enron disclosures, the Bush White House resisted calls to reform accounting procedures, for example, by requiring firms to deduct the cost of executive stock options from reported profits.

Cheney's No-Bid Money Machine

In May 2002 the Securities and Exchange Commission (SEC) opened an inquiry into the accounting practices of the oil services firm Halliburton, headed by Cheney from 1995 to 2000. The SEC found that Cheney, in 1998, had engineered the acquisition of a rival firm despite its asbestos liabilities. Halliburton shares appreciated, and Cheney sold his holdings for nearly $40 million in mid-2000. When the full scale of the asbestos liabilities became known, however, Halliburton stock fell in July 2002 to one-third its value when Cheney unloaded his shares. Was Cheney stupid for not assessing the seriousness of the asbestos problems before the acquisition? Or a knave for keeping them quiet until he bailed out? Or both?

Halliburton remained a major Pentagon contractor, even as its former boss served as U.S. Vice President and received up to $1 million each year from Halliburton in "deferred compensation." Halliburton subsidiary KBR (Kellogg, Brown & Root) received no-bid contracts to rebuild Iraq's oil industry and to build and service U.S. military facilities. Audits showed in December 2003 that KBR had overcharged the Pentagon $61 million for gasoline it imported from Kuwait and $67 million for dining halls built in Iraq. Meanwhile, Halliburton enjoyed an open-ended, cost-plus 1 percent contract to provide U.S. base facilities from the Philippines to Yemen as well as Iraq—an arrangement not calculated to minimize costs.

Circumventing the Constitution

Without obtaining Senate or Congressional approval, President Bush in late 2001 announced that the United States would withdraw from the 1972 Treaty on Antiballistic Missiles. Thirty-three members of the House of Representa-

The WHISTLE-BLOWER-IN-CHIEF ...

The Miami Herald

MORIN

BUK!

HALLIBURTON NO-BID CONTRACT $

SPIN PATROL

CHENEY

YOU'RE FIRED

FEDERAL EMPLOYEES:

NO EMBARRASSING REVELATIONS OR CRITICISM OF BUSH ADMINISTRATION IS PERMITTED (OR ELSE)

tives sued the president, charging that he was violating the Constitution, because abrogating a treaty—part of the highest law of the land—requires Congressional action. Within six months of

Bush's withdrawal statement, however, the United States, for all practical purposes, ceased to be party to the treaty signed by President Nixon thirty years earlier.

The Constitution gives Con-

gress the power to write the laws and obliges the president "to take care that the laws be faithfully executed." Bush, however, asserted he did not need to "execute" a law he believes limits his presidential powers. Bush seldom used the veto, but quietly claimed the authority to disobey more than 750 laws enacted since he took office. He claimed the power to set aside any statute passed by Congress when it conflicts with his interpretation of the Constitution. Previous presidents occasionally used such devices, but Bush challenged more sections of bills than all his predecessors combined—including a ban on torture. Bush also said he could ignore affirmative action provisions, requirements that Congress be told about immigration services problems, and "whistle-

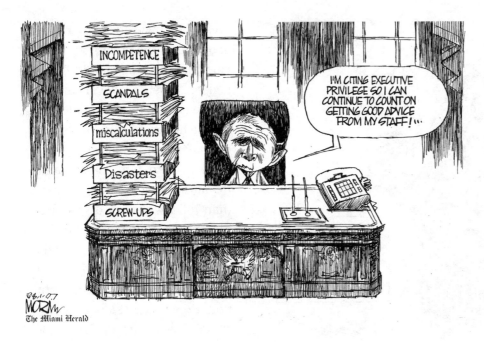

INCOMPETENCE

SCANDALS

miscalculations

Disasters

SCREW-UPS

I'M CITING EXECUTIVE PRIVILEGE SO I CAN CONTINUE TO COUNT ON GETTING GOOD ADVICE FROM MY STAFF! ...

The Miami Herald

blower" protections for nuclear regulatory officials.

Not just Democrats but also the American Bar Association and major legal scholars said the president was breaching the Constitu-tion's separation of powers. But Bush did not bow. On signing the National Defense Authorization Act for 2008 in late January, the president asserted that four sec-tions of the bill unconstitutionally infringed on his powers, and so the executive branch was not bound to obey them. One section forbade spending taxpayer money "to establish any military installa-tion or base for the purpose of providing for the permanent sta-tioning of United States Armed Forces in Iraq" or "to exercise United States control of the oil re-sources of Iraq." This provision aimed to prevent the president from concluding an executive agreement with Iraq's Prime Min-ister that could bind future presi-dents by a compact not defined as a treaty requiring the Senate's approval and consent. House Speaker Nancy Pelosi rejected "the notion in his signing state-ment that he can pick and choose which provisions of this law to execute." Indiana University law professor Dawn Johnson opined that "Congress clearly has the authority to enact this limitation of the expenditure of funds for permanent bases in Iraq."

Bush's January 2008 signing statement also targeted a provision in the defense bill that strengthens protections for whistleblowers working for companies that hold government contracts. Bush also challenged a section that required intelligence agencies to turn over "any existing intelligence assessment, report, estimate or legal opinion" requested by the leaders of the House and Senate armed services committees within forty-five days. Finally, Bush objected to a section establishing an independent, bipartisan "Commission on Wartime Contracting in Iraq and Afghanistan" to investigate allegations of waste, mismanagement,

and excessive force by contractors.

The signing statement, said Harvard law professor David Barron, showed that the White House was still pressing to establish that the commander in chief can defy laws limiting his options in national security matters—as it did also in recent disputes over warrantless wiretapping and interrogation methods. This, said

Barron, was "a dramatic departure from the American constitutional tradition."

Firing Federal Prosecutors

The Justice Department fired seven federal prosecutors on December 7, 2006, and replaced them with interim appointees under the 2005 Patriot Act. Each prosecutor had been appointed by President Bush and confirmed by the Senate four years earlier. But Attorney General Gonzales gave no explanation for their dismissals, saying only that U.S. attorneys "serve at the pleasure of the president." Critics said the firings were politically motivated: Some of the attorneys had failed to impede investigations of Republican politicians; others did not initiate investigations that could damage Democratic politicians.

Gonzales at first denied that he or other top administration officials had been involved. On March 13, 2006, the attorney general said that his deputy, D. Kyle Sampson, had been in charge. But Sampson soon resigned and then testified that his boss lied: The "decision makers" had been the attorney general and the White House Counsel Harriet E. Miers. Sampson claimed he had discussed the firings at least five times with Gonzales; that Karl Rove and other senior White House officials were involved; and that some of the firings were influenced by GOP political concerns. Sampson revealed, for example, that New Mexico U.S. Attorney David C. Iglesias was added to the dismissal list after presidential adviser Rove complained about him. Iglesias later said that Senator Pete V. Domenici and Representative Heather A. Wilson, both New Mexico Republicans, had pressured Iglesias before the midterm elections to probe corruption charges against state Democrats.

Another attorney let go was Carol Lam in Southern California. The *San Diego Union-Tribune* on January 21, 2007, reported that Lam's work "was widely hailed in a region" as that of "a fearless prosecutor taking on the local establishment." But her investigations also reached Washington. She secured the conviction of Randall "Duke" Cunningham (R-CA), "ace" navy pilot and San Diego's longtime representative, jailed in March 2006 for eight

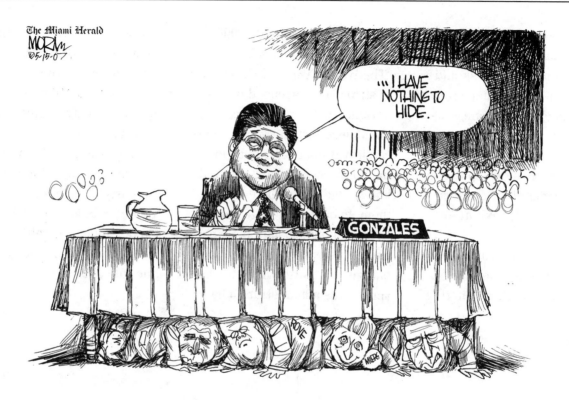

years for fraud, for tax evasion, and for accepting at least $2.4 million in bribes. Before she was fired, Lam also secured the indictment of number-three at the CIA,

Kyle "Dusty" Foggo, after he admitted helping his high school buddy from San Diego Brent R. Wilkes to win CIA contracts. Wilkes, a San Diego defense con-

tractor, has been under investigation for allegedly bribing the Duke. In 2007 Foggo was charged with fraud, conspiracy, and money laundering.

Republican as well as Democratic lawmakers lost confidence in Gonzales and said he should go. President Bush blamed political mudslingers for baseless attacks on Gonzales, his friend from Texas days and longtime coach on how to sidestep the law, but the president let Gonzales make an ungraceful exit in August 2007.

The Bush administration's disdain for the law reached wide and deep, as historian Eric Foner wrote in a December 3, 2006, *Washington Post* article titled "The Worst Ever": "He has sought to strip people accused of crimes of rights that date as far back as the Magna Carta in Anglo-American jurisprudence: trial by impartial jury, access to lawyers, and knowledge of evidence against them. In dozens of statements when signing legislation, he has asserted the right to ignore the parts of laws with which he disagrees. His administration has adopted policies regarding the treatment of prisoners of war that have disgraced the nation and alienated virtually the entire world. Usually, during wartime, the Supreme Court has refrained from passing judgment on presidential actions related to national defense. The Court's unprecedented rebukes of Bush's policies on detainees indicate how far the administration has strayed from the rule of law."

Homeland Insecurity

"Congress gave me the authority to use necessary force to protect the American people, but it didn't prescribe the tactics."

—George W. Bush
defending what he called
a "terrorist surveillance program,"
January 22, 2006

HOW DID America become a nation that tortured prisoners, spied on its citizens, and gave its president unchecked powers in matters of defense?

A strong state may provide security but at what price? Unless people submit to an all-powerful sovereign, said Thomas Hobbes, life will be "nasty, brutish, and short." He called for a "leviathan" to curb the chaos that ensues when every person tries to provide for his own security. Hobbes wrote in the midst of a civil war that racked seventeenth-century England. Later English writers such as John Locke disagreed with Hobbes. They did not defend absolute, but limited, government. America's founding fathers took their inspiration from Locke and other political philosophers who valued freedom as well as order.

What is the best way to provide homeland security for twenty-first-century America? And what is the right price? What should be the trade-off between security and other values—freedom of thought, movement, expression?

Caught napping and stung by 9/11, the Bush team thought it could charge a high price to provide security against more terrorist attacks. The price would not be high in dollar terms, but Americans would have to get used to a big brother whose watchful eye and computerized memory registered every move of every potential terrorist. Big brother would, of course, begin with Muslims but go on to keep files on average U.S. citizens and on all foreigners

GIVE ME YOUR METAL DETECTORS, YOUR FRISKS, YOUR LUGGAGE SEARCHES, YOUR I.D. SPOT CHECKS, YOUR SCARED PEOPLE YEARNING TO FEEL SAFE.

who had any dealings with the United States.

Why Do They Hate Us?

From January through early September 2001, George W. and his inner circle ignored warnings from counterterrorist chief Dick Clarke and the CIA that an al-Qaeda attack inside the United States could well be imminent. America's leaders could have been impeached for sleeping on the job. Instead, the Bush team capitalized on 9/11 to portray the president and his Republican comrades as the necessary bedrock of security. Instead of just cutting the weeds and riding his bike around Crawford, the 43rd president would lead America in a war against terror.

Curiosity about the other side did not figure in Bush's policies at home or abroad. Here was a real blind spot in homeland security. So far as the public record shows, no top official in the Bush administration posed the questions: "Why are so many so intent on attacking us?" "Could we change their views if we changed our policies, for example, on Saudi Arabia or on Palestine?" Instead, the president asserted that the terrorists were out to destroy America's freedoms. The administration used a heavy hand. It tried to spy on everybody and batten down the hatches. The administration gave no sign it considered any other way to buttress homeland security than to eavesdrop, inspect handbags, and build a wall against Mexico.

But the president's assumption was far too simplistic. A study of terrorism around the world found that—from Sri Lanka to Ireland to Palestine—"turf" and dignity were at stake. Terrorists terrorized those who, they thought, occupied or defiled their territory. Unless Washington understood and acted on this, its policies would invite more attacks.

After 9/11 the president quickly approved a CIA plan to overthrow the Taliban regime that harbored al-Qaeda in Afghanistan. Unknown to the public and most government officials, Bush also used 9/11 as a pretext to start planning an attack on Saddam Hussein. In a series of memos and policy decisions, many top secret and made public only much later, the administration's lawyers dismissed the Geneva Conventions as "quaint"; justified the torture of suspected terrorists; argued that the commander in chief was bound by no laws in defending the nation at home and abroad; and approved a domestic surveillance program that violated U.S. law.

Less Safe and Less Free

Bush was slow to accept recommendations from Congress to establish a cabinet-level Department of Homeland Security. He relented, however, and the DHS was established in November 2002. Its job is to protect the territory of the United States from terrorist attacks and respond to natural disasters. By 2008 it had grown to more than two hundred thousand employees—making it the third largest department after Defense and Veterans Affairs.

Once the Department of Homeland Security was established, big brother could operate through the DHS as well as the Justice Department, the FBI, and other federal agencies. Vice President Dick Cheney, often sparked by his counsel David Addington, shaped policy. Bush's counsel, Alberto Gonzales, seemed ready to call "legal" whatever the president wanted.

The Bush administration wanted to prevent more terrorist attacks, but it also realized that it could play on public fears to win approval for virtually any action said to "beef up security." Bush's adviser, Rove, made these assumptions explicit to Republican insiders before the 2004 election.

If the White House became embarrassed by some issue, the DHS could and sometimes did raise its security alert from yellow to orange.

The sound and fury over homeland security led to conditions where Americans suffered the worst of both worlds: They be-

came "less safe and less free." All in the name of preventing future attacks, the administration cut corners on the rule of law—from "water-boarding" detainees, to disappearing suspects into secret CIA prisons, to attacking Iraq "preemptively." Ashcroft oversaw the "preventive detention" of more than five thousand foreign nationals. Many were arrested in secret, without charges, held without any evidence that they were dangerous or a flight risk, denied access to lawyers and the courts, tried in secret immigration hearings, physically beaten by guards, and held for months.

Another Ashcroft invention, the USA PATRIOT Act, allows the government to obtain records from any business, school, or library on U.S. citizens, without showing that they are suspected

The Miami Herald

of criminal activity. It frees the government in many investigations from the requirement that it establish probable cause of criminal activity before it searches a home or taps a phone.

The attorney general unleashed the FBI to spy on political and religious gatherings, even where there was no reason to believe that any criminal conduct was being planned or advocated. Just as

Ashcroft equated criticism of his efforts with treason, his FBI equated antiwar rallies with terrorism. Ashcroft launched the most extensive campaign of ethnic profiling in the United States since Japanese were rounded up in World War II. He called in eighty thousand for registration, fingerprinting, and interviews simply because they came from Arab and other Muslim countries, and sought out eight thousand more for FBI interviews on the same basis. Virtually all the five thousand detained foreign nationals were Arab or Muslim.

Homefront Insecurity

The upshot was that 9/11 saved and then made Bush's presidency—until 2005 when the DHS and its Federal Emergency Management Agency botched its response to Hurricane Katrina in New Orleans. As *USA Today* put it on September 5, 2005: Their "bungled response [to Katrina] should serve as an alert to the rest of the nation. After spending four years and tens of billions of dollars since 9/11 on 'all-hazards preparedness,' FEMA's parent, the Homeland Security Department, failed its first major test."

Hurricane Katrina hit Florida on August 25 and killed thirteen hundred people as it moved across Alabama, Mississippi, and Louisiana, striking New Orleans early on August 28. On September 1, President Bush said, "I don't think anyone anticipated the breach of the levees"—a statement DHS Secretary Michael Chertoff agreed with three days later. On September 3, President Bush assured his audience in Mobile that "out of this chaos is going to come a fantastic Gulf Coast, like it was before." He thanked the faith-based groups and all the others who were working to save lives and rebuild. He especially thanked FEMA director Michael Brown, whom he appointed Under Secretary of Emergency Preparedness and Response and administrator of FEMA in 2003:

> Again, I want to thank you all— and, Brownie, you're doing a heck of a job. The FEMA director is working 24 (applause) they're working 24 hours a day. Again, my attitude is, if it's not going exactly right, we're going to make it go exactly right. If there's problems, we're going to address the prob-

lems. And that's what I've come down to assure people of.

"Heck of a job" soon became sarcastic slang for things done very poorly. "Brownie," like many Bush appointees, was chosen for his politics—not his expertise. Prior to joining the DHS/FEMA, Brown worked for twelve years as commissioner of the International Arabian Horse Association, before being forced out after numerous lawsuits filed against the organization. Only when the dimensions of the Katrina debacle could no longer be denied did the president on September 12 accept Brown's resignation. To head up reconstruction for New Orleans the president then dispatched his number-one PR man, Karl Rove. Given Rove's concern with PR, one thousand firemen recruited from Utah and elsewhere to provide emergency relief on the Gulf Coast were first diverted to Atlanta to be trained as "community relations officers for FEMA."

If big brother were all-knowing and benevolent, perhaps his incursions on personal freedoms would have been more tolerable. But the Bush administration's response to Katrina underscored not just the fallibility but also its narrow values and sheer ineptitude. Complacency operated side by side with wishful thinking and denial. The White House hoped that the levees would hold at New Orleans and later claimed not to have heard that they were cracking. After the waves rushed in, officials in Washington asserted that conditions for displaced people in the Superdome were just fine—even when television screens told a far different story. The plutocracy's insouciance about poor and middle-class Americans also contributed to the catastrophe. A dollop of racism may also have played a role. Many poor people—mostly blacks—were left to drown or swim for their lives. A review of the evidence, according to Joseph Lieberman, the ranking Democrat in a Senate investigation, showed that "government at all levels was forewarned of the catastrophic nature of the approaching storm and did painfully little to be ready to evacuate, search, rescue, and relieve."

Katrina inflicted $150 billion worth of damage to the Gulf Coast region, making it the worst disaster in U.S. history. In the two years after Katrina struck, Congress appropriated $116 billion

The Miami Herald

for Gulf Coast recovery but had designated just $34 billion for long-term rebuilding. And less than half that amount had made its way through federal checks and balances to reach municipal projects. *USA Today* reported on August 29, 2007, that Gulf Coast residents were "asking why their government—at every level—hasn't done more to streamline the process and bring more rebuilding dollars to the region."

Homeland Security Report Card

The United States did not suffer a major terrorist incident after 9/11, but "why" was unclear. The Bush administration may have been either skillful or lucky or both in its efforts to guard America. Osama bin Laden may have preferred to concentrate on Iraq and bide his time before attacking the United States again. But surveys of the DHS by a variety of outside reviewers found a Katrina-like syndrome permeating the organization.

The nonpartisan commission that investigated 9/11 delivered a final report on December 5, 2005, evaluating how the DHS and other branches of government had implemented the commission's recommendations. It gave a set of failing or near failing grades to most of the concerned government agencies. Tellingly, Homeland Security got a D for international collaboration on borders and document security and checked bag screening. Homeland also got two Fs—for radio spectrum for first responders and for critical infrastructure assessment.

The 9/11 commission also faulted intelligence reform. Intelligence oversight reform got a D as did governmentwide information sharing and the oversight of privacy and civil liberties. The establishment of a director of national intelligence and the National Counterterrorism Center scored a B. The FBI national security workforce, however, got a C. The unclassified topline intelligence budget got an F because it remained classified.

In September 2007 the DHS got another set of grades—this time from the Government Accounting Office. The GAO said, in effect, that the DHS dreamed a good game but performed not very well. The GAO concluded that "the department still has much to

The Miami Herald

do to ensure that it conducts its missions efficiently" while preparing for new challenges.

"Preventive Paradigm" Errors

In *Less Safe, Less Free: Why America Is Losing the War on Terror,* David Cole and Jules Lobel argue that the "preventive paradigm" adopted by the Bush administration not only undermined the nation's character but also made the United States more vulnerable to terrorist attacks. The paradigm posits that the government should act preemptively against suspects and check out the evidence later.

The preemptive approach led directly to the detentions at Guantánamo, the use of coercive interrogation and torture, and the

invasion of Iraq. There is no evidence that the paradigm of prevention thwarted actual terrorist plots or captured many terrorists, while there is substantial evidence that it has made Americans less safe.

Cole and Lobel proposed an alternative preventive strategy that favored noncoercive measures,

page 115

multilateral cooperation, and support for the rule of law. America can prevail against the threat of terror, they said, not by dismantling the checks and balances that guarantee the fairness of its justice system, but by restoring them.

In line with this logic, the Supreme Court in June 2008 ruled five to four that the Military Commissions Act of 2006 did not deprive Guantánamo detainees of the right to challenge their detentions in federal court. The majority held that "petitioners may invoke the fundamental procedural protections of habeas corpus. The laws and Constitution are designed to … remain in force, in extraordinary times."

THE GREAT WRIT

THE GREAT HALF-WRIT

The Miami Herald

"The people of the United States and our friends and allies will not live at the mercy of an outlaw regime that threatens the peace with weapons of mass murder."

—George W. Bush
on March 19, 2003, as U.S. forces
began military operations in Iraq

GEORGE W. BUSH'S foreign policy was driven by the politics of preemption. It helped to bring on what is being called the greatest foreign policy disaster in U.S. history. The Bush administration's expedition into Iraq proved destructive not only for Americans and Iraqis but for all whom it touched worldwide. Although few Americans died in Iraq relative to Vietnam, the consequences of the Iraq war will likely prove far more harmful to U.S. interests than Vietnam. The Bush adventure alienated America's longtime admirers and partners and contributed to a global clash between Western and Islamic cultures. It helped turn the United States into the world's largest debtor and helped make energy a hugely expensive commodity for every oil-importing nation. It left thousands of American veterans wounded in mind as well as in body.

Responding to 9/11, the president pledged a "crusade" against the terrorists—a word that reminded Muslims of long wars waged in times past. Bush soon retracted the offending term and sought to distinguish terrorists from good Muslims. Still, he called for a global war against terror. Working with Afghans from the north, the United States quickly overthrew the Taliban regime in Kabul but failed to block Osama bin Laden's retreat into Pakistan.

Why Iraq?

Instead of destroying bin Laden and consolidating a new government in Afghanistan, the Bush team opted to attack Iraq and remove Saddam Hussein from power.

The vice president pressed the CIA to find links between al-Qaeda and Saddam Hussein and evidence that Saddam was acquiring nuclear, biological, and chemical weapons of mass destruction (WMD).

How and why did the White House choose to strike first? The 43rd president may have wanted to avenge his father or show him that his firstborn son was stronger and more decisive than Poppy. The president seemed to think that America and his administration were chosen by God to

spread their values. Underlying this claim was lust for oil plus ignorance of the cultures and societies to be "liberated." Three men close to the throne—Vice President Cheney, Defense Secretary Rumsfeld, and his deputy Paul Wolfowitz—saw Saddam Hussein as an obstacle to their long-standing goal of making America's military so strong that no other player could dream of challenging U.S. hegemony. All four wanted to complete the job unfinished in 1991 when the first President Bush halted the U.S. offensive that could have led from Kuwait to Baghdad.

Lies to Mask Lies

CIA director George Tenet assured Bush it would be a "slam dunk" to prove the WMD threat from Iraq, but the National Intelligence Estimate presented to the White House in October 2002 found no clear links between al-Qaeda and Saddam.

It stated only that Iraq was *seeking* nuclear weapons and trying to reconstitute the biological and chemical programs that had been destroyed during and after the 1991 Gulf War. Later claims that the CIA had transmitted erroneous info were untrue—a cheap trick to blame bad White House decisions on bad intelligence. The White House cherry-picked the NIE and other intelligence reports for evidence that America needed to strike "preemptively" against Saddam.

The House and Senate in October 2002 authorized the president to attack Iraq if Saddam Hussein refused to give up his WMD. How did the Bush administration persuade Congress and the public to go along? In essence, it lied. A staff study conducted for Rep. Henry A. Waxman (D-CA) found that, between March 2002 and March 2004, Bush and his four aides—Vice President Cheney, secretaries Powell and Rumsfeld, and National Security Adviser Rice—made 237 misleading statements about the threat posed by Iraq, its WMD capabilities, and its links to al-Qaeda. Most of the misleading statements about Iraq were made prior to the start of the war—sixty-seven in the month before Congress voted to authorize an attack. But seventy-six misleading statements were made after the start of the war to justify the decision to go to war. Thus, Cheney insisted on January 22, 2004: "There's overwhelming evidence that there was a connection between al-Qaeda and the Iraqi government."

Confidence in the patriotism as well as the integrity of the Bush administration got a jolt in July 2003 when former ambassador Joseph Wilson disclosed that the Bush administration had misled

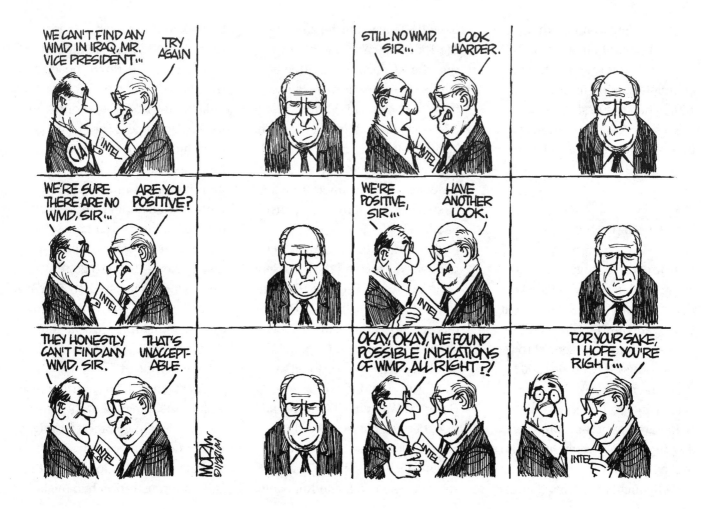

the public by suggesting that Iraq had sought to obtain uranium in Africa. Wilson said that the CIA had sent him to Niger to check out this story, and he reported that it had no basis in reality. Accordingly, he expressed shock when Bush included this allegation in his January 28, 2003, State of the Union address. A week after Wilson's disclosure, columnist Robert Novak reported that Wilson's wife, Valerie Plame, was a CIA "operative" on WMD. Since it is unlawful to disclose the iden-

tity of CIA agents, demands came from many quarters to learn who had leaked this information to Novak. The White House denied any involvement. But an investigation revealed that Cheney's top aide, I. "Scooter" Libby, had lied about his role. A jury convicted Libby of obstruction of justice, perjury, and making false statements to federal investigators.

Libby was the highest-ranking White House official convicted in a government scandal since 1990 when Reagan's security adviser, John Poindexter, was convicted of multiple felonies in the Iran-Contra affair. Bush soon commuted Libby's sentence, but the "Plame affair" did not end there. White House press secretary Scott McClellan said he had been duped on this matter by Bush, Cheney, Rove, and Libby. An excerpt from McClellan's memoir, *What Happened*, was posted on the Web site of PublicAffairs Books in November 2007. McClellan wrote that:

> The most powerful leader in the world had called upon me to speak on his behalf and help restore credibility he lost amid the failure to find weapons of mass destruction in Iraq. So I stood at the White House briefing room podium in front of the glare of the klieg lights for the better part of two weeks [in October 2003] and publicly exonerated two of the seniormost aides in the White House: Karl Rove and Scooter Libby.
>
> There was one problem. It was not true.
>
> I had unknowingly passed along false information.

Mission Accomplished?

Deploying fewer than two hundred thousand troops, the U.S.-led invasion toppled Saddam's regime within weeks in spring 2003 and Bush declared "Mission Accomplished!" As experts on the Middle East had predicted, however, Iraq's tribal society proved extremely difficult to rule. L. Paul Bremer III, U.S. administrator for reconstructing Iraq from May 2003 to June 2004, opted to disband the Iraqi army and prevent any former members of Saddam's Baathist party from taking jobs in the new administration. Missing the chance to rechannel the patriotic energies of educated Iraqis, proconsul Bremer instead created a virtual army of disaffected and unemployed men—many of them armed. Asserting that "stuff happens," Rumsfeld did nothing to prevent or halt pillaging of Iraqi museums and the sites where a shared civilization began more than four millennia ago.

At first some Iraqis welcomed the incursion by U.S. and British forces. Soon, however, the ensuing chaos produced a sense of great insecurity and resentment. Iraqis turned against the foreign occupiers and then against one another. Battle lines and allegiances shifted like desert sands.

Violence increased in 2006. Some thirty-five thousand Iraqis

died thanks to criminality, insurgency, and sectarian violence. General George Casey tried to shift more responsibility to Iraqi forces, but the U.S.-led "coalition" then lost control of many areas it had previously stabilized. As conditions in Iraq deteriorated, the Iraq Study Group headed by James Baker and Lee Hamilton recommended in December 2006 that the White House seek to enlist Syria and Iran to help stabilize Iraq. President Bush paid lip service to this recommendation and permitted some exchanges with diplomats from Damascus and Tehran. But Bush's major response was to order in January 2007 a "surge" of thirty thousand additional troops tasked with pacifying Baghdad and winning hearts and minds. Violent deaths decreased in Iraq in the second half of 2007, but the situation remained a powder keg. A month or two of relative calm could be followed by increased violence. The Iraqi government reported that 633 civilians died violently in February 2008, much less than the previous year but a 36 percent increase over January 2008. Most Democrats in Congress wanted

a deliberate withdrawal of U.S. forces, but Republican presidential candidate John McCain said the United States should stay in Iraq for another hundred years if need be.

Truth and Consequences

The invasion into Iraq achieved none of its advertised objectives but generated a Hydra of grave new challenges:

Heightened Nuclear Danger to the United States

Americans found (as the United Nations did before them) that Iraq possessed no nuclear weapons. Focused on Iraq, the Bush administration did almost nothing to halt nuclear developments in North Korea and Iran.

Only after Pyongyang's first nuclear test in 2006 did Washington negotiate seriously with North Korea.

Loss of Credibility at Home and Abroad

If the administration—even Colin Powell—had deceived Americans and the United Nations, how could anyone trust the Bush team to speak the truth on anything?

A Straited Military

The neocon dream of unchallenged hegemony collapsed as Iraq devoured the human and material resources of the U.S. military. The American juggernaut proved vulnerable to asymmetric warfare. Exhausted and embarrassed by its shortfalls in Iraq, America's forces no longer looked unbeatable. Recruitment standards slipped and bonuses increased as the Pentagon grew desperate to enlist volunteers for a hazardous and perhaps futile operation.

Alliances Sundered

Washington could no longer count on NATO. The United

States expended far more than 4 percent of GDP on defense; most other NATO countries, less than 2 percent. Some NATO countries sent troops to Afghanistan, but many placed their forces far from harm's way. Most NATO partners refused to send troops to Iraq. Donald Rumsfeld's "coalition of the willing" was a joke. In 2008 there were more than 155,000 American troops in Iraq and some

10,000 from other "coalition" members. Estonia, Latvia, and Slovakia provided two soldiers each; Slovenia and Ukraine sent three.

Civil Strife

The American presence and some U.S. policies ignited ancient animosities among Iraq's Sunni minority and Shiia majority. Kurds in the north demanded autonomy if not independence. Some leaders, clans, and factions within each group tried to exterminate each other. Some fought Americans for a time and then leagued with them against local rivals.

Greater Leverage for Tehran

Iran gained the most from the fall of Saddam. The U.S. administration permitted the long marginalized Shiia majority to gain the upper hand in post-Saddam Iraq. Not only did Shiia share the faith and shrines of most Iranians, but many of their leaders had found refuge in Iran during the Saddam years. Now Iran could back this or that Shiia faction with money, arms, and know-how.

The Miami Herald

Human Suffering

After five years of fighting, more than four thousand U.S. soldiers had died and thirty thousand were wounded—many incapacitated for life. There were no reliable estimates of Iraqis killed or wounded since 2003. Estimates ranged from one hundred thousand to nearly seven hundred thousand killed. By 2008 there were more than 2 million Iraqis displaced within the country and another 2 million displaced to neighboring countries—from a population of 27.5 million.

Economic Burdens

The Bush team had predicted that defeating and rebuilding Iraq would cost less than $60 *billion*. Instead, the total costs to Americans are likely to exceed $3 *trillion* and could approach the $5 trillion (inflation-adjusted) expended in World War II. This estimate, by Nobel economics laureate Joseph E. Stiglitz and Harvard professor Linda J. Bilmes, includes the obvious burdens neglected by White House propaganda such as the long-term costs of caring for injured veterans; interest on war debts not paid from current revenues; and death benefits to mercenaries as well as regular troops. Stiglitz and Bilmes suggest that the Iraq war also helped bring on the 2007–2008 economic crisis. The Federal Reserve tried to offset the adverse effects of the war by lowering interest rates, but this helped bring on the subprime debacle when interest rates later rose. The Bush administration used every trick in the book to hide the real price tag—concealing noncombat casualty figures, keeping double sets of books, not factoring in support troops, and allowing the Pentagon to produce budgets so contradictory and obscure that few if any persons knew what outlays were planned or took place.

Of course the impact on Iraq's economy was worse—and beyond measure. Chaos in Iraq also harmed economies around the globe. One barrel of oil cost about $25 in 2003. Five years later it topped $140. This increase hurt not only Americans but also Europeans, Chinese, Indians, and all who relied on imported oil. The corresponding rise in the petrodollar hoards of Saudi Arabia, Russia, Venezuela, Nigeria, and other unsavory regimes did nothing to advance the causes of freedom and security.

Psychological Costs

Americans lives were disrupted by separations and anxiety for loved ones, anguish over those

killed and wounded, and fear of returning vets with murder on their minds. Some 30 percent of returning vets faced serious mental health problems. Divorce rates climbed in military families. Millions of Iraqis faced even worse situations. Many lost hope as education and careers were cut short. Many who could flee Iraq—physicians and other professionals— did so. The United States, however, admitted very few—even those who had risked everything serving as interpreters and guides.

An Increased Terrorist Threat to America

Bush justified the Iraq expedition as a way to fight the terrorists over there and keep them from U.S. shores. But he created a maelstrom of terrorist activity where little or none has existed before. Of course Saddam Hussein had been a menace to his own people and to Iraq's neighbors Iran and Kuwait, but not to the United States or Europe. Indeed, the United States had helped Saddam Hussein during his eight-year war against Iran. With Saddam gone and Americans occupying Iraq, the country became a recruiting and training ground for anti-American Islamist militants the world over.

To gain perspective, we can do no worse than to look (with humanities professor Daniel Mendelsohn, in *The New Yorker*, April 28, 2008) at the "father of history," Herodotus, and what he tells us about another great empire, Persia. Led first by a father and then, a decade later, by his son, this great power twice invades a smaller, strange, and faraway land—Greece, expected to be an easy target. The father is "a bland and bureaucratic man, far more temperate than the son." The second invasion, led by the son, is on a far larger scale than the first, and ends in disaster. Some commentators ascribe the disaster to the flawed decisions of a man "whose bluster competes with, or perhaps covers for, a certain hollowness at the center; a leader who is at once hobbled by personal demons (among which it seems is an Oedipal conflict), and given to grandiose gestures[;] . . . incapable of comprehending . . . [or worse] incurious about . . . his enemy." While the son is "unscathed by the disaster he has wreaked, the fortunes and reputation of the country he rules are seriously damaged."

The Miami Herald

An Intensified Clash of Civilizations

Beginning with the time when marines first landed on "the shores of Tripoli" to fight the Barbary pirates, America's conflicts with the Arabic world have arisen primarily from economic and political issues, and not from any clash of cultures or religions. But Bush's policies deepened the perceived fault-lines between the West and Islam. Muslims saw the U.S. occupation of Iraq as another Crusade against their faith. They ignored U.S. support for Muslims in Bosnia, Kosovo, and Macedonia and the efforts of former President Jimmy Carter and other U.S. leaders in behalf of Palestinians. Many despised the United States for aligning not only with Israel but also with some of the most repressive leaders in Islamic countries—from Saudi Arabia to Pakistan. Goaded by their own highly inflammatory media and many mullahs, many Muslims joined or approved jihad against the West. For now, most Muslims could wage only asymmetric warfare and terror attacks on the West. Some Muslim states possessed the oil weapon and its economic leverage. One—Pakistan—had nuclear weapons. Some day there might be more.

"This bill spells out specific, recognizable offenses that would be considered crimes in the handling of detainees so that our men and women who question captured terrorists can perform their duties to the fullest extent of the law.

And this bill complies with both the spirit and the letter of our international obligations. . . . [T]he United States does not torture. It's against our laws, and it's against our values."

—George W. Bush
on signing the Military Commissions
Act of 2006, October 17, 2006

In wartime, "anything goes" replaces respect for law and morality. Bad becomes good or, at the least, necessary. Deception, hate, and cruelty are virtues. This tendency is not new. Thucydides described it in Greece some twenty-four hundred years before George W. Bush became president. Still, many U.S. presidents of both parties have tried to limit what "goes" in wartime—*at least until 2001.*

On March 6, 1991, President George H. W. Bush called for efforts to build a new world order in which "justice and fair play . . . protect the weak against the strong." The elder Bush followed in the footsteps of other Republicans—Theodore Roosevelt (Nobel Peace Laureate in 1906), William Howard Taft (League to Enforce the Peace, 1915), Warren G. Harding (Washington Naval Limitations, 1922), Herbert Hoover (Pact to Renounce War, 1928), Dwight D. Eisenhower (Spirit of Geneva, 1955), Richard N. Nixon (SALT, 1972), Gerald Ford (Helsinki Final Act, 1975), and Ronald Reagan (INF Treaty, 1987). Democratic presidents also contributed to these efforts— Woodrow Wilson (League of Nations, 1919), Franklin Roosevelt (United Nations, 1945), Harry Truman (Marshall Plan, 1947; NATO, 1949; and in Korea, 1950), John F. Kennedy (nuclear test ban, 1963), Jimmy Carter (Camp David Accords, 1978), and Bill Clinton (Dayton Accords, 1995).

The younger president Bush, however, spat on his father's and America's heritage and relied on brute force to get his way in the world. He tore up the Anti-Ballistic Missile Treaty (ABMT) signed by Nixon—and did so without consulting Congress. He refused to ratify the Kyoto Protocol, which had been signed but not ratified under Clinton. Bush "unsigned" America's founding signature on the International Criminal Court. He named John Bolton the U.S. ambassador to the United Nations—a public figure so hostile to the UN that his appointment could not win approval by senators of either party.

The Bush administration threw America's legal traditions to the winds and replaced them with a manifest disdain for law and morality at home and abroad. Treaties, as the Constitution says, are part of the "supreme Law of the land [article vi.2]." For Bush, however, international commitments were only sheets of paper, easily shredded. The Bush team interpreted U.S. obligations to suit its convenience. Administration efforts to deny legal protections to suspected terrorists worried U.S. military officers and others concerned that Americans taken on some future battlefield would get similar treatment.

Guantánamo Bay

Throughout history, prisoners have been enslaved, executed, and ransomed. To protect wounded combatants, POWs, and civilians during times of war, a series of "Geneva Conventions" were adopted prior to World War II and expanded in 1949 and

1977. But the emergence of powerful militants acting not for a state but on their own or for a "non-state" movement created a situation with few recent precedents. U.S. government lawyers called these actors "illegal enemy combatants." To ensure that persons who had been captured and were suspected of being "illegal enemy combatants" had no rights under U.S. law, the Pentagon placed 759 of them in Guantánamo, Cuba—leased but not a U.S. territory.

For many observers, Guantánamo symbolized American oppression. However, international pressures on Washington brought some changes. Following a Supreme Court ruling, the Department of Defense accepted that Guantánamo detainees are entitled to protection under the

Geneva Conventions. Some prisoners no longer considered a threat were released. Others were repatriated. In 2007 some detainees began to appear before U.S. military tribunals. In mid-

2008 this left some 270 detainees deemed by the U.S. authorities to pose a continuing danger, whose own governments would not accept them, and for whom no obvious solution existed. Bush said he

would like to see the facility closed, but this seemed unlikely under his administration.

In October 2007, Col. Morris Davis resigned as chief prosecutor for Guantánamo Bay's military commissions because, he thought, "full, fair and open trials were not possible under the current system." He quit just hours after he learned he was to be placed under the command of President Bush's appointee and alleged torture advocate William J. Haynes. Following the recent military prosecutors' decision to seek the death penalty for six Guantánamo detainees to be charged with central roles in the 9/11 attacks, Davis stated he did not believe "the men at Guantánamo could receive a fair trial." Davis recalled that in August 2005 he mentioned to Haynes that "at

Nuremberg [Nazi war crime trials] there had been some acquittals, which had lent a great credibility to the proceedings." Haynes replied, "Wait a minute, we can't have acquittals. If we've been holding these guys for so long, how can we explain letting them get off? . . . We've got to have convictions." Confirming this state of mind, Clive Stafford Smith, an attorney who has represented more than seventy Guantánamo detainees, noted that three prosecutors had requested to be transferred out of the Office of Military Commissions in 2004 after being "told by the chief prosecutor at the time that they didn't need evidence to get convictions."

With regard to suspected terrorists who are U.S. citizens, President Bush claimed he possessed the right to hold them without trial indefinitely. He saw himself as above the law or, rather, as the law. Like Richard Nixon, Bush seemed to believe that, if the president did something, that made it legal.

"Extraordinary Rendition"

As part of the war on terror, the CIA moved—"rendered"—some suspected terrorists to third countries for detention and interrogation without going through formal judicial processes. Some European and Middle Eastern governments colluded with the CIA, but the Council of Europe and the European Parliament investigated these practices. Their reports, published in 2006 and 2007, concluded there had been as many as twenty-one cases of extraordinary rendition by the CIA and a substantial number of CIA flights in and out of Europe between 2001 and 2005, to transport subjects of extraordinary rendition. Separately, an Italian prosecutor issued arrest warrants for twenty-three CIA officers accused of kidnapping an Egyptian cleric in Milan in 2003. Prosecutors in Germany, Spain, and Portugal opened investigations into other cases of extraordinary rendition.

"Extraordinary rendition," author Salman Rushdie observed in 2005, was the "ugliest phrase to enter the English language." The "phrase's brutalisation of meaning is an infallible signal of its intent to deceive." Here the meaning of extraordinary was stretched "to include more sinister meanings that your dictionary will not provide: secret; ruthless; and extra-judicial." Of seventeen dictionary meanings for rendition, one cannot find "to kidnap and covertly deliver an individual or individuals for interrogation to an undisclosed address in an unspecified country where torture is permitted." The calculated blandness of the U.S. government's usage "makes us shiver with fear—yes, and loathing." Writing in the *Sydney Morning Herald*, January 10, 2006, Rushdie agreed with *New York Times*'s columnist William Safire's view that "clean words can mask dirty deeds"—referring to the arrival of another such phrase, "ethnic cleansing," in 1993. Squeamish officials used Orwellian doublespeak such as "final solution" and "mortality response" (killing) to hide a brutal reality. Similarly, they employ extraordinary rendition to mask "export of torture."

Faced with protests from European allies, Secretary of State Rice was not squeamish. She asserted in 2005 that rendition was "a vital tool in combating transnational terrorism." Washington did not apologize for using "black" detention facilities, the existence of which was confirmed by Bush in September 2006.

"Enhanced" Interrogation Techniques

Torture is forbidden by specific U.S. laws as well as by the Geneva Conventions. Still, some authorities say that torture may sometimes be necessary to save lives. Against this rationalization, many experienced interrogators say that torture rarely produces useful information. There are other drawbacks as well. Information obtained in this way may not be used in courts. If the United States uses enhanced techniques, other governments may be less willing to cooperate against terrorists. Instead of intimidating terrorists, stories of such techniques may stimulate recruitment into terrorist groups. Americans some day may also be tortured.

During Bush's "war on terror," U.S. interrogators used a variety of "enhanced" methods of interrogation such as sleep deprivation, stress positions, face-slapping, and "waterboarding"—pouring water over a person's face to simulate drowning. Waterboarding seldom kills, but it is both painful and frightening and can damage

the lungs and brain. Most legal experts and human rights activists regard waterboarding as torture.

A Justice Department memorandum dated August 1, 2002, to Alberto Gonzales, then the White House counsel, stated that U.S. law permits a wide range of interrogation techniques short of those that cause extreme pain or death. The U.S. Code (Section 2340) implementing the Geneva Convention on Torture imposes criminal penalties only for torture—not for "cruel, inhuman, or degrading treatment." A second memorandum, dated March 14, 2003, instructed the Pentagon that the military could ignore the Geneva Conventions and the War Crimes Act passed by Congress when interrogating "enemy combatants." Neither Fifth Amendment due process guarantees nor Eighth Amendment prohibitions against cruel and unusual punishment "extend to alien enemy combatants held abroad." Further, "federal criminal law" may not be applied to "interrogations of enemy combatants, undertaken by military personnel in the course of an armed conflict" because that would be an unconstitutional infringement on executive branch power.

When numerous instances of "sadistic, blatant, and wanton criminal abuses" of Iraqi prisoners by U.S. military and intelligence officials at the Abu Ghraib prison in 2003 were exposed, the world recoiled in horror. Photos, videos, and detailed witness testimony painted a picture of U.S. violations that were difficult to deny. Given the license granted by the Justice Department memoranda, however, it is little wonder that such violations occurred.

The "two torture memos," as they became known, were drafted by John C. Yoo, who subsequently left "Justice" in to teach law (!) at the University of California, Berkeley. Both memoranda were formally withdrawn in 2004 by Jack L. Goldsmith, who took over briefly as the director of the Office of Legal Counsel. Goldsmith concluded that legal opinions on torture, warrantless surveillance by the National Security Agency, and related issues were fundamentally flawed—"a legal mess." In 2004 a watchdog agency within the Justice Department, the Office of Professional Responsibility, began to investigate whether "the legal advice contained in those memoranda was consistent with the professional standards that apply to department of Justice attorneys."

Earlier attempts to hide waterboarding, in particular, evoked wide concern in January 2008. Michael B. Mukasey, who replaced Gonzales as attorney general in 2007, assigned a special U.S. attorney to investigate whether CIA officials committed crimes by destroying interrogation videotapes of two high-level al-Qaeda detainees, including one who was waterboarded. However Mukasey rebuffed demands from Congress to investigate the interrogations themselves, saying officials were acting under legal advice from the Justice Department.

Playing his maverick role, Senator John McCain deftly referred to his own heroic past and urged Congress to ban torture by the

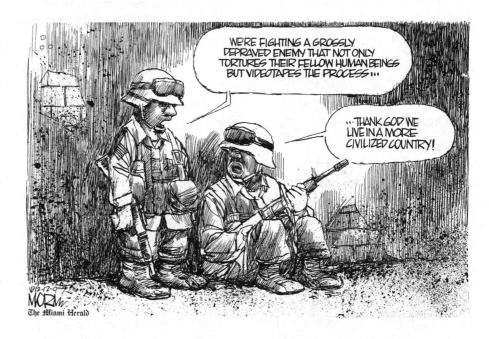

The Miami Herald

U.S. military. In October 2005 Congress banned the use by the military of "cruel, inhuman, or degrading interrogation techniques." The Bush administration countered that it did not employ "tor-

ture" and insisted that the CIA be allowed to use waterboarding.

McCain waffled big time. On October 25, 2007, the Arizona Republican said that waterboarding "is a terrible and odious practice

and should never be condoned in the U.S."—implying it is okay in Guantánamo and other non-U.S. locations. Indeed, in January 2008, McCain spoke out against a bill that required the intelligence community to adhere to the same rules as the U.S. Army Field Manual, which—as revised—banned waterboarding. McCain then voted against the bill, which passed the Senate 51–45, on February 13, 2008. McCain urged Bush to veto the measure and, in March, Bush did just that.

Law and Order at Home and Worldwide

The Bush administration's willingness to torture and "render" suspected terrorists derived from a confidence that it stood above the law. The administration's heavy reliance on coercion achieved more negative than positive results. Its reputation as a brutal lawbreaker added to the many reasons why foreigners as well as Americans did not trust the Bush administration. This was bad not only for the United States, but for all humanity, because the Bush team pulled away the foundations of a world order that had been painfully erected in the previous century. It also increased the risk that American POWs would be tortured.

CHAPTER
11

Democracy?

The Miami Herald

"Because we have acted in the great liberating tradition of this nation, tens of millions have achieved their freedom. And as hope kindles hope, millions more will find it."

—George W. Bush
second inaugural address,
January 20, 2005

GEORGE W. BUSH assumed the presidency at a time of high hopes for democracy and human rights. The United States had become the sole superpower—respected for its moral appeal as much as for its material might. The death of communism a decade earlier, according to political philosopher Francis Fukuyama, meant "the end of history," i.e., that liberal democracy had triumphed worldwide. Princeton professor Michael Doyle observed that no established democracy had ever attacked another. If Fukuyama and Doyle were right, humanity was entering a golden age. Harvard political scientist Samuel P. Huntington, however, warned that a clash of civilizations was underway.

George W. paid little heed to fancy theories but said in 2000 that the United States should conduct a modest foreign policy and avoid "nation-building." But then September 11 changed everything. Humility went out and was replaced by intervention. Having found no weapons of mass destruction in Iraq, the Bush administration justified the U.S. presence there in different terms. America, Bush promised, would democratize the Middle East and bolster human rights, thereby destroying the spawning grounds of terrorism. The White House predicted a domino effect. Once democracy took root in Iraq, it would spread across the region.

These hopes soon proved naïve. Many people in Iraq *did* want self-rule and braved brazen threats to cast their votes. But most Iraqis voted along sectarian lines. The largest group, Shiia Muslims, dominated the new government. Its soldiers and police routed many Sunnis from their homes and forced them to flee. Since democracy requires not just majority rule but also respect for minorities, Saddam's successors got off to a bad start.

Analysts for Freedom House, a non-partisan think-tank in New York, recorded little improvement in the freedom rankings of most Middle Eastern countries following the U.S. occupation of Iraq. That country was not free in 2000 but still not free in 2008. The curbs on Iraqis' political rights and civil liberties were different from those under Saddam Hussein, but were still quite severe.

Two neighbors, Turkey and Kuwait, were partly free in 2000 and remained partly free in 2008. Two other neighbors, Syria and Iran, were not free in 2000 and remained not free in 2008. Further along the Persian Gulf, the United Arab Emirates and Saudi Arabia were not free in 2000 and remained not free. Afghanistan and Lebanon moved from not free to partly free, but each wrestled with severe problems. Egypt, Tunisia, and Jordan initiated political reforms in the 1980s, but these reforms lost momentum or were undone. Tunisia moved back to rigid authoritarianism, and Egypt became less free. Though relatively calm, Morocco spawned the masterminds of the Madrid train explosions and many volunteers for al-Qaeda in Iraq. The only outpost of democracy

"THE DESIRE FOR FREEDOM RESIDES IN EVERY HUMAN HEART."

"AND THAT DESIRE CANNOT BE CONTAINED FOREVER BY PRISON WALLS, OR MARTIAL LAWS, OR SECRET POLICE."

"OVER TIME, AND ACROSS THE EARTH, FREEDOM WILL FIND A WAY..."

—BUSH TO U.N., 2004

MORIN

The Miami Herald

"...MAYBE NEXT YEAR..."

U.S. ALLY

PAKISTAN

in the region was Israel—ranked free for decades, despite living under siege.

What Went Wrong?

Why did Bush's democracy campaign founder? For starters, the United States under Bush was a poor model. Bush took the presidency in two deeply flawed elections and then ran the country to benefit a narrow stratum. Second, his campaign for democracy abroad was clearly an afterthought. Third, democracy cannot be readily exported or imposed from the top down. The foundations for a functioning democracy are lacking in most Arab countries. The Arab world may need its own version of the Protestant

Reformation, but no "Martin Luther" is in sight.

Bush's repeated justification of the Iraq war as a democratizing mission discredited some Western-oriented Arab democrats.

Many Arabs came to view democracy itself as a code word for U.S. regional domination. The unpopularity of the war and the abuses against Iraqis at Abu Ghraib further tarnished the reputation of

the United States and fueled Islamist extremism.

Israel and Its Neighbors

Israel's occupation of Palestinian lands aggravates the conditions inimical to democracy and human rights and undermines U.S. efforts to reform the region. As the Iraq Study Group Report, chaired by James Baker and Lee Hamilton, warned in December 2006: "The United States cannot achieve its goals in the Middle East unless it deals directly with the Arab-Israeli conflict and regional instability."

A great power with greathearted leaders can help other actors tamp down and, sometimes, resolve their conflicts. President Theodore Roosevelt mediated the

The Miami Herald

Russo-Japanese War in 1905 and used his influence to calm a French-German confrontation over Morocco in 1906. The first American black to win the Nobel Peace Prize was UN mediator

Ralph Bunche, who brokered the 1949 armistice between Israel and its neighbors. Secretary of State Henry Kissinger used shuttle diplomacy to stabilize the 1973 Arab-Israeli ceasefire. Jimmy

Carter in 1978–1979 brokered a peace treaty between Egypt and Israel. Carter repeatedly walked between the cabins of Israeli Prime Minister Menachem Begin and Egyptian President Anwar Sadat to broker the Camp David Accords in 1978.

Each mediation showed how a third party can help disputants find an accommodation that advances the interests of each side. Helping others, Roosevelt, Kissinger, and Carter also raised America's stature; and Bunche, that of the United Nations. Other U.S. officials and presidents tried to mediate but with less success. Secretary of State James Baker and his successor Warren Christopher tried to bridge Arab-Israeli differences but achieved no breakthroughs. Bill Clinton, too, tried but failed. George W. Bush,

however, hardly tried. Unlike most of his predecessors, the 43rd president showed little interest in helping others mend their disputes. His hands-off stance permitted tensions in the Middle East to go from bad to worse.

Why did Bush stay so aloof? His disdain for diplomacy was reinforced by the American Israel Public Affairs Committee (AIPAC) and other elements in the Israel lobby. The lobby multiplied its strength by aligning with Christian Zionists rooting for a climactic victory of good over evil. Working with neocon policy wonks such as Richard Perle and Douglas Feith, the lobby kept much of Congress as well as the White House in its pocket. If Bush's peace rhetoric soared, the lobby brought him back to earth. Israel and its lobby strongly en-

couraged the Bush administration to invade Iraq. Later, they pushed for a U.S. attack on Iran.

The Road Map and the Fence

In 2002–2003 the Bush administration laid out a "road map" for a two-state solution to resolve the Israeli-Palestinian problem. The Israeli government and Palestinian leader Mahmoud Abbas endorsed the road map but with serious reservations. The map placed great emphasis on "compliance," but did not define compliance or spell out the consequences for noncompliance. Bush predicted the road map would lead to an accommodation in three years—a quick fix for a complex tangle.

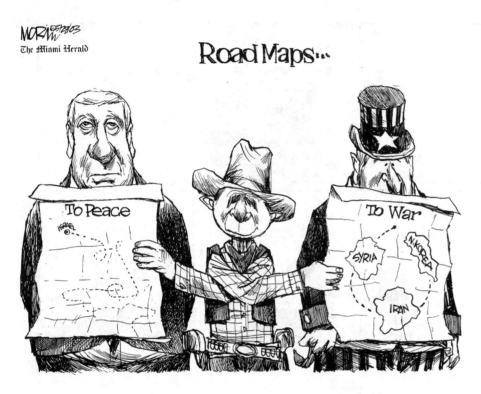

MORIN 05/28/03
The Miami Herald

Road Maps...

To Peace

ISRAEL

To War

SYRIA

N.KOREA

IRAN

violated Israel's obligations as an occupying power.

Following Yasser Arafat's death in November 2004, both Washington and Israel welcomed the election of Mahmoud Abbas, a moderate within Fatah, as president of the Palestinian Authority. But the same month Abbas was elected—January 2005—also saw the victory of the Hamas faction in municipal elections in Gaza. The Arab TV station Al Jazeera explained that Gazans rejected Fatah's corrupt image and endorsed Hamas for its opposition to Israel and for its welfare services. In September 2005 Israel evacuated all Jewish settlers from Gaza. Although the Bush administration stumped for self-rule, it scorned the Hamas government elected by Gazans. This stance encouraged Hamas to play the spoiler—sabo-

As Bush announced his road map, however, Israel began to construct a wall to seal off the West Bank from Israel. Washington offered only mild objections but the International Court of Justice in July 2004 advised the UN General Assembly that the wall taging every prospect of a deal between Abbas and Israel.

The next year, 2006, hostilities erupted between Hezbollah and Israel, further undermining the road to reconciliation. Seeking to wipe out Hezbollah, strongly backed by Iran, Israel assaulted its strongholds in Lebanon. Israel's attacks lacked proportionality, but Washington blocked UN efforts for a ceasefire. Indeed, President Bush on July 18, 2006, endorsed Israel's campaign to cripple Hezbollah. He accused Syria of intervening in Lebanon and called for isolating Iran. But Hezbollah survived, and Israel backed down—arguably Israel's first defeat by Arabs. Some said America's puppet now looked like a paper tiger. The failure of Israeli arms buoyed Iran's claim to leadership of the Muslim world.

As the U.S. occupation of Iraq became ever more problematic, the Bush White House looked for success elsewhere. The Baker-Hamilton Study Group Report in late 2006 recommended that Washington open channels with Iran, but some administration hawks wanted to attack Iran and change its regime. Robert Gates succeeded Rumsfeld as secretary of defense in November 2006 and cautioned Bush that U.S. forces were stretched too thin to take on Iran.

If action against the ayatollahs was not feasible, the president wanted to scoop victory from the jaws of defeat elsewhere. Bush renewed his calls for a quick-fix, two-state solution for Israel and Palestine. Accordingly, Secretary of State Rice made many trips to the Middle East and arranged a *one-day* (!) summit of interested parties in Annapolis, Maryland, in November 2007. Despite strong rhetorical commitments, however, the Bush administration did not follow through. The contrast with Camp David in 1978 was telling. On that occasion Carter cajoled Begin and Sadat for thirteen days. At Annapolis, Bush gave one speech that broke no new ground. He called again for a two-state solution but did not suggest any possible compromises, such as making Jerusalem the capital for both states. He called Israel a "a homeland for the Jewish people"—implying that the Arab diaspora had no right to return.

As Bush's second term ended, the road vanished. Abbas had lost control of Gaza where the population had elected leaders opposed to peace with Israel and to Abbas, whom they called a traitor. Israel had pulled out of Gaza but continued to expand settlements in lands that Palestinians regarded as theirs. Rice in 2008 called the expansions "unhelpful" but U.S. support for Israel did not waver.

Almost Everyone Loses

Ending their standoff depended ultimately on Arabs and Israelis, but the Bush administration's one-sided and half-hearted interventions nearly guaranteed that no accommodation would be reached. The failure of the United States to help resolve the Arab-Israeli confrontation kept America from gaining credibility as an advocate of democracy. Liberal Arabs said the U.S. campaign for democracy is rank hypocrisy—manifested in indifference to the rights of Palestinians and unconditional support for Israel. The impasse left America and the Middle East with many dire consequences, especially considering that Iran became stronger as the fortunes of others—especially Palestinians in Israel—declined.

The United States lost influence and respect—not just in the Middle East, but worldwide.

Freedom Diminished

The number of countries that Freedom House judged "free" in 2007 stood at 90, representing 47 percent of the world's 193 polities and 46 percent of the global population. For the first time in fifteen years, global freedoms declined two years in a row—in 2006 and 2007. Many of the worst abusers of human rights were (or had been) chummy with the Bush administration—Russia, Georgia, Azerbaijan, Pakistan, Egypt, Nigeria, Kazakhstan, Uzbekistan, and Kyrgyzstan.

Bush's erstwhile friend Vladimir Putin laid waste to Russia's

incipient democracy and built a police state—key ministries and provinces headed by his former comrades in the KGB. Journalists were intimidated or murdered and Putin waged a genocidal war in Chechnya. Indeed, most of the former Soviet Union became a democratic wasteland. Except for the democracies in Estonia, Latvia, and Lithuania, there were just a few shaky pockets of pluralism, such as the Ukraine.

A large swath of East and Southeast Asia—from North Korea and China down through Vietnam, Laos, and Burma—was a democracy-free zone with few prospects for democratic change. Malaysia went from free to partly free, thanks to a decline in religious freedom and restrictions on the press. Singapore was rich but not very free. In Pakistan, Benazir Bhutto was assassinated in the context of a state repression and Islamic extremism. China cracked down on Tibetans and other minorities as well as democratic reformers. Beijing also helped authoritarian regimes in Africa and Burma. It forcibly returned escapees to North Korea.

What to Do?

Promoting democracy throughout the Middle East will require doing away with fantasies of a sudden U.S.-led transformation of the region. It will demand rebuilding U.S. credibility in Arab eyes. Democracy is not a quick-fix remedy for terrorism.

Fear? Indoctrination? Apathy? Whatever the reasons, many Americans were ready to accept government censorship in 2008. A survey of public opinion in twenty countries in early 2008 found that 22 percent of Americans wanted the press to have less freedom—a share exceeded only by India (32 percent). Nearly a quarter (24 percent) of Americans thought the government should have the right to prevent people from having access to some things on the Internet—about the same percentage as in China (23 percent) and twice the share in Azerbaijan (12 percent). Some 88 percent of Americans thought it important for the media to publish news and ideas without government control—a bit more than in China (85 percent) but less than in Peru, Egypt, Nigeria, or South Korea (see www.worldpublicopinion.org, accessed May 12, 2008).

Probably the best way Americans can foster democracy is to practice it at home. That—and developing a foreign policy of global respect and inclusion—could go a long way toward reversing the current democratic demise.

And instead of demanding that all humanity mimic the United States, the next White House might instead pursue the guideline suggested by Harlan Cleveland, a former U.S. ambassador to NATO, "to place our power in the service of a world of diversity," in his 1966 book, *The Obligations of Power: American Diplomacy in the Search for Peace.*

12

The Bush Doctrine

"If we wait for threats to fully materialize, we will have waited too long."

—President George W. Bush
commencement address at
West Point, June 1, 2002

THREATS TO "security" can arise from within or outside the country. They can arrive in many forms—not just as bullets, bombs, and rockets, but also as disease, food shortages, and climate change. Poor education and health care also endanger national as well as individual security. A wise government will organize resources to cope with these many challenges. It will cultivate societal fitness, the ability to coerce and persuade, plus the wisdom and skill to cope with and reduce external threats. Its diplomacy will utilize soft as well as hard power to counter military dangers.

The Eagle on the Great Seal of the United States carries an olive

signed by presidents Nixon in 1972, Carter in 1979, Bush the Elder in 1991 and 1993, and by George W. Bush in 2002.

Antagonizing China and Russia

The greatest large-scale military threats to Americans come from China and Russia, but the Bush team in its first nine months treated both countries with near contempt. Instead of fostering co-operation with China, the White House emphasized China's role as a strategic rival, while virtually ig-noring the erstwhile Russian su-perpower. Things changed after 9/11 as Washington sought Chi-nese and Russian help in the war against terror. Bush then ignored human rights abuses in China and

branch as well as thirteen arrows. Arms control as well as arms can enhance security. This reality has been a constant in U.S. policy

from the 1817 Rush-Bagot Accord on Great Lakes disarmament to the 1922 Washington Naval Con-ference to strategic arms treaties

Russia in return for their acquiescence in U.S. bases in Central Asia.

Even after 9/11, however, the Bush team planned for the worst with Beijing and Moscow. The Pentagon's *Nuclear Posture Review* in January 2002 said Washington would no longer regard nuclear weapons as a last resort. Instead, U.S. strategists would plan for contingencies in which America might use nuclear weapons against seven or more adversaries. The list began with the "axis of evil" trio—Iraq, Iran, and North Korea—but also included Libya, Syria, Russia, and China. The United States might use nuclear weapons to retaliate against chemical or biological weapons attacks, hit targets able to withstand conventional weapons, or deal with "surprising military developments." Smaller nukes might be used to bust bunkers such as al-Qaeda's presumed mountain headquarters.

The Bush strategic plan looked naïve. It aspired to minimize "collateral damage" while using nuclear weapons against hard targets. It counted on cruise missiles and drones to destroy enemy forces without much need to fight them on the ground, occupy defeated lands, or rebuild defeated countries. It promised aseptic war—trouble-free and virtually painless for Americans. The president's national security adviser, Condoleezza Rice, said the United States could not wait until a mushroom cloud appeared. The vice president said that if there were just a "one percent chance" some foe planned to attack America with WMD, the United States should preempt. Dr. Rice noted that President Kennedy had "thought about a lot of possibilities," including a preemptive strike, against Soviet missiles in Cuba. In response, Kennedy's special counsel Ted Sorensen acknowledged that JFK had "thought about" a preemptive strike but had then rejected this option. JFK did not want to kill civilians without warning; risk a wider war; and lose the moral high ground.

"The trouble with a preemptive strike doctrine," Sorensen said, "is that it preempts the president's own choices." In the twenty-first century there were other drawbacks. If the United States sought a capacity to preempt, China and Russia would probably intensify their own arms buildups. Other countries—perhaps Pakistan and India, China and India, Israel and Iran—might follow the American example. Already in 2003 the one percent doctrine led to disaster. Bush claimed his war on Iraq aimed to preempt its WMD ambitions, but this was a deceptive misnomer. The assault aimed to *prevent* Iraq from obtaining WMD—not to *preempt* an imminent attack.

The Miami Herald

Destroying the Most Important Arms Limitation of All Time

President Bush signed the Strategic Offensives Reduction Treaty (SOR) with Russian President Putin in 2002.

Uncomfortable with legalisms, Bush had preferred a declaration of intent but finally agreed to a formal document just three pages long—quite a contrast to the hundreds of pages in some earlier U.S. treaties with Moscow. That same year, however, Bush effectively reversed the momentum toward lowering the role of nuclear weapons in U.S.-Russian relations. He declared that the United States was withdrawing from the 1972 treaty limiting antiballistic missile defenses. He did so even though many experts judged the ABM treaty the most important arms limitation of all time because it permitted the two supers to cap their offensive weapons arms race. If its rival had only limited defenses, each side could feel secure with a smaller deterrent. This logic permitted Washington and Moscow to freeze and then reduce their nuclear systems.

Bush's missile defense plan pushed the old allies, Russia and China, together again. Each cautioned Washington that it would take countermeasures. But Bush pulled out of the ABM treaty and initiated deployment of a fledgling ABM system in Alaska and California. As Putin's government

had warned, it refused to ratify the Strategic Arms Reduction Treaty (START II) signed in 1993, which banned multiple nuclear warheads. Without this restraint,

each side could make a joke of arms treaties by placing several—even a dozen—warheads atop each missile.

Later, when Putin learned that

the United States wished to deploy elements of its antimissile defenses in the Czech Republic and Poland, he "suspended" Russian participation in the 1990

Conventional Forces in Europe Treaty and threatened to aim Russian missiles at Eastern Europe. China also intensified efforts to improve its small but potent mis-

sile force. Displaying an ability to blind the Pentagon, China shot down one of its own aging satellites—a tacit warning to other space warriors.

When Bush met Putin in Sochi in April 2008, neither side gave way on any strategic issue. As before, they agreed to enact nuclear weapons reductions "to the lowest possible level consistent with our national security requirements and alliance commitments." But Moscow wanted a new treaty limiting both strategic warheads and delivery vehicles, while the Bush administration preferred an agreement focused on codifying some verification measures to last beyond the scheduled 2009 expiration of the 1991 Strategic Arms Reduction Treaty (START). Even so, Bush wanted to count only "operationally deployed strategic" warheads in any future treaty, which meant each side could keep undeployed missiles in reserve.

Ignoring the Number One Threat to the Nonproliferation Treaty

There was no way that the nascent Alaska-California network could do much against an attack by a thousand Russian missiles or even a few dozen Chinese. The network had never been tested as an integrated system. Tests of system components usually failed unless they were rigged. Many scientists thought it impossible the system could ever distinguish nuclear warheads from decoys.

The only nuclear threat that might be neutralized by America's ABM force was that of North Korea. Kim Jong-il's regime thus served as the main justification for a defense system that deeply agitated Moscow and Beijing. However the system's potency against North Korea was also doubtful. If Pyongyang could launch nuclear-tipped ICBMs, it could also send up decoys. (An SM–3 missile fired from the *SS Lake Erie* in November 2007 intercepted and destroyed two unitary, nonseparating targets; another shot down an ailing U.S. satellite in February 2008, but these were easy tasks compared to intercepting ICBMs without advanced warning and then distinguishing decoys from real warheads.)

Of the three nations on the "axis of evil" identified by President Bush in January 2002, North Korea was the closest to acquiring a nuclear weapons and missile capability. Iraq's efforts in this direction were demolished after the 1991 Gulf War, while Iran's nuclear programs lagged North Korea's by at least a decade.

Following his ABC rule—"Anything But Clinton"—Bush aborted the promising negotiations with North Korea begun in the 1990s. Rejecting "carrots," Washington also forswore "sticks." Bleeding from the Iraq war, the Pentagon began to siphon U.S. troops from South Korea to staunch the flow. All this gave reason for Pyongyang to go nuclear.

The Bush team refused to talk with North Korea in 2001. It insulted Pyongyang and its "dear leader" in 2002. It did nothing to save the 1994 U.S.–North Korean Agreed Framework, which kept

Pyongyang from producing a plutonium bomb. Washington refused to meet one-on-one as North Korea wished but, somewhat reluctantly, took part in the six-party talks sponsored by Beijing, starting in 2003. Meanwhile, North Korea withdrew from the Nuclear Nonproliferation Treaty and expelled international inspectors.

Only after North Korea tested a nuclear device in 2006 did the United States get serious about negotiations. In 2007 North Korea agreed to disable the facility from which it obtained plutonium and by year's end to document all its other nuclear facilities. In December 2007 it refused to follow through on this second step, complaining that Washington had so far provided only one-fourth the fuel oil it had promised as a quid

pro quo. Permitting North Korea to go nuclear ranked high among the foreign policy failures of the Bush years. Hopes rose for a broad accommodation with North Korea when, in May 2008, Pyongyang handed over thousands of pages describing its past nuclear activities—minus any mention of uranium enrichment or a Syrian connection. Whether the horse could ever be put back in the barn, however, remained unclear.

U.S. policy toward Iran was equally mindless. Initially shocked and awed by America's quick victory over Saddam Hussein, Tehran in 2003 proposed talks on all the issues separating Iran and the United States. Swelling with pride, Washington refused. When Washington later asked Iran to help calm Iraq, the Iranians raised their terms.

What Do We Spend on Defense? What Do We Get for It?

On Bush's watch, the official defense budget grew to exceed military spending in all other countries combined. The White House said that the Defense Department budget, plus nuclear weapons research in the Department of Energy, consumed some 4 percent of GDP—twice the NATO average but less than during the Korean War or the peak years of Vietnam engagement.

The White House statistics failed, however, to include spending on spy satellites and other intelligence activities; military dimensions of NASA; the soaring costs of veterans' benefits; foreign aid (International Security Assistance); or many outlays for

The Miami Herald
MORIN 9/18/01

the vast network of U.S. bases abroad. The White House reckoning omitted three whoppers: (1) The costs of ongoing operations in Afghanistan and Iraq—$142 billion in 2007; (2) interest payments on America's total debt, of which at least one-third derived from previous military activities; and (3) Homeland Security. Including these additional costs, the total burden of defense was closer to 8 than to 4 percent. This was another instance of sleight-of-hand manipulation of facts to create fictions. If we add the *indirect* as well as the direct costs of the Iraq War, such as the economic dislocations, the impact on trade, and the rising price of oil, the true burden of defense probably approached one-tenth of GDP.

Apart from big increases in the regular Defense Department budget, the International Institute for Strategic Studies reckoned that military *operations* in the Afghan and Iraq wars and for Homeland Security cost American taxpayers more than $600 billion through mid-2007. The total outlays forecast by Joseph E. Stiglitz and Linda J. Bilmes, as noted earlier, exceed $3 trillion.

175

What did Americans get for these outlays?

- Participation in an elective war, with no end in sight, that alienated much of humanity and inspired volunteers for an expanded jihad;
- An overstretched military unable to meet the post–Cold War goal of being able to fight and win two regional wars while carrying out a substantial humanitarian operation.

As Gen. George Casey, U.S. Army Chief of Staff, put it: "Current demand on our forces exceeds the sustainable supply. . . . We are consuming our readiness as fast as we are building it."

- Increased determination and action by Beijing and Moscow to take down the "sole superpower" from its pedestal;
- The emergence of another nuclear-armed state, Kim Jong-il's North Korea, while Iran continued efforts to produce nuclear weapons-grade fuel;
- A weakening of arms control regimes to halt nuclear proliferation, contain and damp down strategic arms competition, and keep the terrestrial arms race from outer space;
- Failure to do anything to prevent genocide in Darfur and conflict in other troubled areas.

13

The Bush Legacy

"It is no surprise that in one of Bush's last acts of relevance, he once again played the fear card. Although he has failed in spreading democracy, stemming global terrorism, and leaving the country better off than when he took power, he did achieve one thing: successfully perpetuating fear for political gain."

—Richard A. Clarke
  former head of counterterrorism
  at the National Security Council,
  Philadelphia Inquirer, February 1, 2008

WHAT DID the George W. Bush administration achieve? Where did it fail? Did it meet its own objectives? Do more good or harm for the country? Perspectives could change as more information appears. Here is a summary based on what is known in 2008.

Democracy ambushed: George W. Bush twice took the presidency. Doing so, however, he damaged faith in the institutions of American democracy.

The economy eroded: Bush-onomics rewarded the president's wealthiest backers but hurt the U.S. economy and material well being of most Americans. Even before defense spending soared, Bush's tax policies transformed

FORWARD PASS '''

The Miami Herald

the budget surpluses achieved in the late 1990s into deficits that will burden us for years—perhaps generations—to come.

Tax cuts for the rich failed to encourage investment and job creation because the purchasing power of most Americans lagged inflation. True, consumers benefited from cheap imports, but their purchases widened the trade gap. America's spending sprees made a debtor nation dependent on China and other foreign lenders. India and other developing countries siphoned jobs from the United States. By 2008 one dollar got you half a euro.

The rich got richer, but most Americans ran hard just to maintain their present living standards. Wages stagnated as prices rose. Housing equity collapsed in 2006–2008.

Laissez-faire was overrated. As Nobel economics laureate Joseph Stiglitz observed, Adam Smith's "invisible hand" is invisible because it does not exist. People and markets need some protection by government. A widening wealth gap puts social stability at risk.

Brain damage: Deteriorating social and cultural conditions undermined education. K–12 schools did not improve when NCLB pressured teachers to teach to the test. Reduced government aid kept more kids from college. Scientists complained their work was underfunded or skewed, censored to fit a right-wing agenda.

Fusing church and state: Determined to keep the support of the Christian right, Bush funneled

The Miami Herald

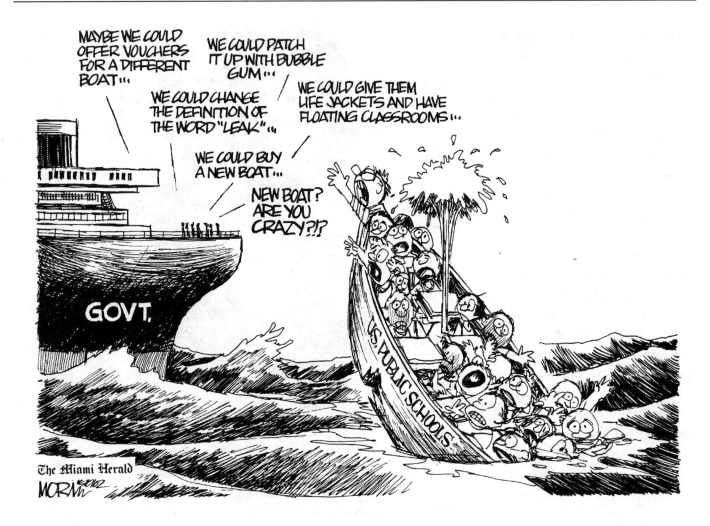

government money to support many faith-based activities. His administration permitted evangelical professors and cadets at the Air Force Academy to haze non-Christians. It banned stem-cell research but labored to keep a Florida woman in a vegetative state for fifteen years on life support. It wanted schools to teach the "theory" of intelligent design alongside evolution.

Health at risk: "The world's best health system" worked miracles for some but let down most

Americans. Americans paid more for health care but died earlier than citizens of Cuba and Costa Rica, not to speak of Japan. Bush did nothing to halt the growing and future demands of health care on the economy. His major health policy innovation helped pharmacopia profit from seniors.

School, street, and home safety: Bush Republicans and some Democrats opposed regulations on guns. For many kids, gun violence made it dangerous to walk to school, listen to the teacher, or stay at home. College professors and students were also at risk, as were strollers on many

city streets. The NRA came through unscathed.

Environmental destruction: The president talked the talk of blue skies, green forests, clean air, and clean water but walked the path of big oil, big coal, and big lumber. His EPA labored to undo the protections of earlier years. Bush promised a "science-based response to the issue of global warming" but rejected the best science on the topic.

Energy dependency: Bush and Congress sustained U.S. dependence on foreign oil by resisting fuel efficiency standards and other conservation measures; by low funding for research into alternative fuels; by subsidizing roads and industrial farming rather than mass transportation and sustainable agriculture; and by supporting corn-based bio-

fuels—an energy and environmental dead end.

Less safe and less free: As the cover of this book suggests, the Bush administration ended up destroying liberty under the guise of saving it. The president flouted the law to eavesdrop and lock up suspects. The Department of Homeland Security was an awk-

ward Rube Goldberg contraption given more tasks than it could hope to fulfill. It failed in New Orleans, where the dangers and problems were obvious. Could anyone trust its ability to cope with the panoply of terrorist options?

Disastrous disaster relief: Indifferent to the dangers from Hurricane Katrina, incompetent in responding to the disaster, slovenly in rebuilding afterwards, the administration helped to lay low a city, its people, and its culture.

Public distrust in the law: The Bush administration twisted or

The Miami Herald

ignored the law to pursue its agenda. The president broke the ABM treaty and enforced other laws as he pleased. If a federal attorney did not follow White House wishes, out she or he went.

Attorney General John Ashcroft and, later, Alberto Gonzales subverted the law more than they implemented it—ditto the Supreme Court.

Openness denied: The Bush team proved itself more secretive than any government in U.S. history. Of course it needed to mask some military devices, tactics against terrorists, and intelligence methods. But the White House

The Miami Herald

often used secrecy to hide information that could embarrass the administration, while it leaked the identity of a CIA operative—a treasonous offense.

Competence and integrity at risk: Ideology + hubris + a focus on enriching the rich = great damage to government's ability to deal with any problem. The Bush administration's nearly willful ignorance often produced horrific results. Reliant on big lies and devoted to fattening Bush patrons, the administration proved less honest than any in more than a century. It lied not only about Iraq—from 2002 through 2008, but about other issues, such as balancing the budget without more taxes.

The TORTURE continues ...

RED INK

①1·7·08
MORIN
The Miami Herald

Counterterrorism: Having done almost nothing against al-Qaeda before 9/11, the administration knocked out its HQ in Afghanistan but then failed to capture its leader. Instead, Bush chose to attack Iraq on false pretenses and depose its dictator. All this embroiled the United States in a long and costly war that made Iraq a recruiting and training ground for terrorists. It gutted efforts to stabilize Afghanistan and Pakistan. The entire enterprise intensified the clash of civilizations. It also wore down the American armed forces, weakened the economy, and diverted

The Miami Herald

the United States from investing in infrastructure and other domestic needs.

Disparaging international rules and restraints: Hostile to domestic law, the administration also inflicted heavy damage on the new world order that the senior George Bush saw emerging in 1991. It assaulted international accords—the Kyoto Protocol, the International Criminal Court, and the Geneva Conventions. Acting like a rogue beast, the Bush administration burned America's credentials as a force for law and order. Its neologisms such as "extraordinary rendition" offended the English language as well as basic morality.

Breaking the edifice of arms control: Confident of U.S. military power, the Bush administration flaunted its willingness and capacity for unilateral action. If there were only a one percent chance some hostile actor planned to attack the U.S. homeland, America would strike first. The Bush team claimed to oppose nuclear proliferation and gave this as the main reason to attack Iraq. But it winked at the nuclear arsenals of friendly powers—Israel, India, Pakistan—and for six years offered neither carrot nor stick to dissuade North Korea from going nuclear. Meanwhile, Washington provided few incentives for Iran to stop enriching uranium.

Failing to try for peace in the Holy Land: For decades the Arab-

MORIN 6/4/03
The Miami Herald

Israeli conflict has festered and occasionally threatened to drag the United States into a major war. The issues are not insurmountable. Both Egypt and Jordan made peace with Israel. But peace in the region requires inten-

sive diplomatic intervention by an even-handed, muscular, and well-endowed mediator. Bush placed a very low priority on this kind of effort—condemning the parties to fight it out. The perceived American tilt toward Israel adds to

The Miami Herald
MORIN 8/3

the motives for anti-American attacks.

Giving democracy and human rights a bad name: Bush's policies in the United States undermined admiration for American democracy. His campaign to democratize the Middle East looked like a rationalization for U.S. occupation of Afghanistan and Iraq. The United States clamored for respect for human rights in Venezuela, Cuba, and Burma. But what about human rights—now—for Palestinians?

Losing friends and inspiring enemies: The Bush team damaged positive relationships with friends and allies built up over decades or even centuries. Its reliance on unilateral military power nearly destroyed America's ability to persuade and coopt. Most NATO countries refused to follow Bush into Iraq or do much to stabilize Afghanistan. China and Russia resolved to build up their own assets to defy and perhaps someday challenge the U.S. hegemon.

Weakening civilization: Most of the great civilizations—at least fourteen out of twenty-one—have disappeared. Most arose as a creative response to a set of complex challenges; most perished from a failure to cope with new challenges. Most of the failures suffered from hubris; most abused their environment, and most wasted resources in imperial overstretch. Most became lazy and hedonistic, unable to repulse barbarians at the gates.

Although living standards and lifespans increase worldwide, two challenges could end all life as we know it—climate change and weapons of mass destruction.

Time could be short. Each threat can be reduced by wise policies already on the drawing

THE OTHER WEAPON OF GLOBAL MASS DESTRUCTION...

POLLUTION

The Miami Herald

boards. But without U.S. leadership to frame and implement these policies, effective action is unlikely. Nothing that Norway or The Netherlands does, for example, will count for much unless the United States goes along. Neither China nor India nor Russia nor Brazil is likely to act unless the United States moves first.

Instead of taking the lead on these challenging issues, the Bush administration made them more difficult to tame.

The Bottom Line

Looking at the Bush record, we see little that is constructive and much that is harmful and even disastrous. It is possible that the Bush administration has been not only the least accomplished but also the most destructive in U.S. history—at home and abroad. When earlier administrations did something harmful, negative impacts were generally localized. Today, when the United States does something good or bad, repercussions travel with Internet speed to all corners of the world.

The Miami Herald

The Bush team ambushed Americans in 2000 but not in 2004. By then, its behaviors were obvious. Still, nearly half of U.S. voters asked for more. It took the Katrina disaster and the endless Iraq War for Americans to perceive that the emperor had no clothes. It is not surprising that dozens or hundreds or even thousands of Americans want to grab power for their own, mostly private objectives. That millions would go along is astounding.

The Bush team got away with

murder. Thousands died to slake its appetite for power and wealth. Millions became poorer and more vulnerable. Calls for impeachment got nowhere—judged unrealistic.

Our earlier book, *Bushed!*, concluded in 2004 that the forty-third president was the worst—at least in the last century. In 2006 Columbia University historian Eric Foner went further. In the December 3 edition of the *Washington Post*, he termed George W. the "worst ever." When the History News Network asked historians in the spring of 2008 to evaluate the Bush presidency, 98 percent of 109 respondents declared it an outright "failure," and more than 60 percent deemed it the worst in the nation's history. Still, nearly half the voters got what they wanted not only in 2000 but also in 2004.

To be sure, one brave soul in Mark Twain's *Connecticut Yankee* doubted that any free voter would "voluntarily get down in the mud" and submit to tyranny. Still, Twain worried that many people are "nothing but rabbits." He felt shame for the human race to "think of the sort of froth that has always occupied its thrones without shadow of right or reason, and the seventh-rate people that have always figured as aristocrats." Twain rather agreed with Connecticut's constitution "that all political power is inherent in the people, and all free governments are founded on their authority and instituted for their benefit."

Relevant Readings

Chapter 1. The Bush Gang

American Presidency Project [database of all public statements by U.S. presidents] at http://www.presidency.ucsb.edu/index.php.

Berlow, Alan. "The Texas Clemency Memos," *The Atlantic* (July/August 2003).

Dubose, Lou. "Don't Mess with Texas," *LA Weekly* (September 16, 2004).

Dubose, Lou, and Jake Bernstein. *Vice: Dick Cheney and the Hijacking of the American Presidency.* New York: Random House, 2006.

Cannon, Carl M., Lou Dubose, and Jan Reid. *Boy Genius: Karl Rove, The Architect of George W. Bush's Remarkable Political Triumphs.* New York: PublicAffairs, 2003.

Ivins, Molly. *Shrub: The Short but Happy Political Life of George W. Bush.* New York: Random House, 2000.

——. *Who Let the Dogs In? Incredible Political Animals I Have Known.* New York: Random House, 2004.

Hargrove, Erwin C. *The Effective Presidency: Lessons on Leadership from John F. Kennedy to George W. Bush.* Boulder, CO: Paradigm Publishers, 2008.

Naftali, Timothy J. *George H. W. Bush.* New York: Times Books, 2007.

Weisberger, Jacob. *The Bush Tragedy.* New York: Random House, 2008.

Chapter 2. Campaigns & Elections

Blumenthal, Sidney. *How Bush Rules: Chronicles of a Radical Regime.* Princeton, NJ: Princeton University Press, 2006.

Brock, David. *The Republican Noise Machine: Right-Wing Media and How It Corrupts Democracy.* New York: Crown Publishers, 2004.

Dubose, Lou, and Jan Reid. *The Hammer: Tom Delay, God, Money, and the Rise of the Republican Congress.* New York: Public Affairs, 2004.

Dye, Thomas. *Who's Running America: The Bush Restoration.* Upper Saddle River, NJ: Prentice Hall, 2002.

Edwards, George C. III and Desmond S. King, eds.; *The Polarized Presidency of George W. Bush.* New York: Oxford University Press, 2007.

Frank, Thomas. *What's the Matter with Kansas? How Conservatives Won the Heart of America.* New York: Metropolitan Books, 2004.

Green, Joshua. "The Rove Presidency," *The Atlantic* (September 2007).

Weisberg, Jacob. "Interest-Group Conservatism," *www.slate.com* (May 4, 2005).

Chapter 3. The Politics of Wealth

Bartlett, Bruce. *Impostor: How George W. Bush Bankrupted America and Betrayed the Reagan Legacy.* New York: Doubleday, 2006.

Chait, Jonathan. *The Big Con: The True Story of How Washington Got Hoodwinked and Hijacked by Crackpot Economics.* Boston: Houghton Mifflin, 2007.

Greenspan, Alan, *The Age of Turbulence: Adventures in a New World.* New York: Penguin, 2007.

Johnston, David C. *Free Lunch: How the Wealthiest Americans Enrich Themselves at Government Expense and Stick You with the Bill.* New York: Portfolio, 2007.

Johnston, David C. *Perfectly Legal: The Covert Campaign to Rig Our Tax System to Benefit the Super Rich and Cheat Everybody Else.* New York: Portfolio, 2003.

Jones, Bryan D., and Walter Williams. *The Politics of Bad Ideas: The Great Tax Cut Delusion and the Decline of Good Government in America.* New York: Pearson Longman, 2008.

Kotlikoff, Laurence J., and Scott Burns. *The Coming Generational Storm: What You Need to Know about America's Economic Future.* Rev. ed.; Cambridge, MA: The MIT Press, 2005.

Ornstein, Norman J. "The House That Jack [Abramoff] Built," *New York Times Book Review*, January 14, 2007.

Stone, Peter H. *Heist: Superlobbyist Jack Abramoff, His Republican Allies, and Buying of Washington.* New York: Farrar, Straus, and Giroux, 2006.

Suskind, Ron. *The Price of Loyalty: George W. Bush, the White House,* and the Education of Paul O'Neill. New York: Simon & Schuster, 2004.

Chapter 4. Faith, Education, & Science

Faith

DiIulio, John J., Jr. *Godly Republic: A Centrist Blueprint for America's Faith-Based Future.* Berkeley, CA: University of California Press, 2007.

Dionne, E. J., Jr. *Souled Out: Reclaiming Faith and Politics After the Religious Right.* Princeton, NJ: Princeton University Press, 2008.

Gushee, David P. *The Future of Faith in American Politics: The Public Witness of the Evangelical Center.* Waco, TX: Baylor University Press, 2008.

Kuo, David J. *Tempting Faith: An Inside Story of Political Seduction.* New York: Free Press, 2006.

Lambert, Frank. *The Founding Fathers and the Place of Religion in America.* Princeton, NJ: Princeton University Press, 2003.

———. *Inventing the "Great Awakening."* Princeton, NJ: Princeton University Press, 2000.

———. *Religion in American Politics: A Short History.* Princeton, NJ: Princeton University Press, 2008.

Phillips, Kevin P. *American Theocracy: The Peril and Politics of Radical Religion, Oil, and Borrowed Money in the 21st Century.* New York: Viking, 2006.

Education and Science

Berry, Tiffany, and Rebecca M. Eddy, eds.; *Consequences of No Child Left Behind for Educational Evaluation.* San Francisco: Jossey-Bass, 2008.

Gore, Al. *The Assault on Reason.* New York: The Penguin Press, 2007.

Hursh, David W. *High-Stakes Testing and the Decline of Teaching and Learning: The Real Crisis in Education.* Lanham, MD: Rowman & Littlefield, 2008.

On education and science in the United States FY 2009 budget. *http://www.ed.gov/about/overview/budget/budget09/factsheet.html.*

Richter, Burton. On federal support for science, at Web site of Scientists and Engineers for America, *http://sefora.org/2008/02/19.*

Sadovnik, Alan R., et al., eds.; *No Child Left Behind and the Reduction of the Achievement Gap: Sociological Perspectives on Federal Educational Policy.* New York: Routledge, 2008.

Sunderman, Gail L., ed.; *Holding NCLB Accountable: Achieving Accountability, Equity, & School Reform.* Thousand Oaks, CA: Corwin, 2008.

Union of Concerned Scientists, "Federal Science and the Public Good," *www.ucsusa.org/scientificfreedom,* February 14, 2008.

Chapter 5.
Health of the Nation

Andersen, Ronald, and John F. Newman, "Societal and Individual Determinants of Medical Care Utilization in the United States," *The Milbank Quarterly* 83, 4 (December 2005).

Busch, Michael. "Is the Second Amendment an individual or a collective right: United States v. Emerson's revolutionary interpretation of the right to bear arms," *St. John's Law Review* (Spring 2003).

CDC National Center for Health Statistics, *Health, United States, 2007, with Chartbook on Trends in the Health of Americans.* Washington, DC: Government Printing Office, 2007.

Cohn, Jonathan. *Sick: The Untold Story of America's Health Care Crisis—and the People Who Pay the Price.* New York: Harper-Collins, 2007.

Feldman, Richard. *Ricochet: Confes-*

sions of a Gun Lobbyist. Hoboken, NJ: John Wiley, 2007.

U.S. Census Bureau, *Statistical Abstract of the United States: The National Data Book.* Washington, DC: Government Printing Office, 2007.

United Nations Development Programme, *Human Development Report* (New York—annual).

Chapter 6. Energy & the Environment

Abraham, Rick. *The Dirty Truth: George W. Bush's Oil and Chemical Dependency: How He Sold Out Texans and the Environment to Big Business Polluters.* Houston, TX: Mainstream Publishers, 2000.

Bush, George W. *A Blueprint for New Beginnings: A Responsible Budget for America's Priorities/ Executive Office of the President of the United States.* Washington, DC: Office of Management and Budget, Executive Office of the

President. Washington, DC: Government Printing Office, 2001.

Campbell, Dowling et. al.; *A Bird in the Bush: Failed Policies of the George W. Bush Administration.* New York: Algora, 2005.

Juhasz, Antonia. *The Bush Agenda: Invading the World, One Economy at a Time.* New York: ReganBooks, 2006.

Loo, Dennis, and Peter Phillips, eds. *Impeach the President: The Case Against Bush and Cheney.* New York: Seven Stories Press, 2006.

Pope, Carl, and Paul Rauber. *Strategic Ignorance: Why the Administration Is Recklessly Destroying a Century of Environmental Progress.* San Francisco: Sierra Club Books, 2004.

Rossi, Melissa L. *What Every American Should Know About Who's Really Running the World: The People, Corporations, and Organizations that Control our Future.* New York: Plume, 2005.

Vig, Norman J., and Michael E. Kraft eds.; *Environmental Policy: New*

Directions for the Twenty-first Century. Washington, D.C.: CQ Press, 2003.

Chapter 7. Secrets of State

Alterman, Eric. *When Presidents Lie: A History of Official Deception and Its Consequences.* New York: Viking, 2004.

Borjesson, Kristina, ed.; *Into the Buzzsaw: Leading Journalists Expose the Myth of a Free Press.* Rev. ed. New York: Prometheus Books, 2004.

Continetti, Matthew. *The K Street Gang: The Rise and Fall of the Republican Machine.* New York: Doubleday, 2006.

Goulden, Joseph C. *The Superlawyers: The Small and Powerful World of the Great Washington Law Firms.* New York: Weybright and Talley, 1972.

McClellan, Scott. *What Happened: Inside the Bush White House and Washington's Culture of De-*

ception. New York: PublicAffairs, 2008.

Rich, Frank. *The Greatest Story Ever Sold: The Decline and Fall of Truth from 9/11 to Katrina.* New York: The Penguin Press, 2006.

Savage, Charlie. *Takeover: The Return of the Imperial Presidency and the Subversion of American Democracy.* New York: Little Brown and Company, 2007.

Schwarz, Fredrick A. O., and Aziz Z. Huq. *Unchecked and Unbalanced: Presidential Power in a Time of Terror.* New York: New Press, 2007.

Shenon, Philip. *The Commission: The Uncensored History of the 9/11 Investigation.* New York: Twelve, 2008.

Signing statements by U.S. presidents, http://www.presidency.ucsb.edu/signingstatements.php.

Chapter 8. Homeland Insecurity

Ackerman, Bruce. *Before the Next Attack: Preserving Civil Liberties in an Age of Terrorism.* New Haven, CT: Yale University Press, 2006.

Ashcroft, John. *Never Again: Securing America and Restoring Justice.* New York: Center Street, 2006.

Baker, Nancy V. *General Ashcroft: Attorney at War.* Lawrence, KS: University Press of Kansas, 2006.

Benjamin, Daniel, and Steven Simon. *The Next Attack: The Failure of the War on Terror and a Strategy for Getting It Right.* New York: Times Books, 2005.

Clarke, Richard A. *Against All Enemies: Inside America's War on Terror.* New York: Free Press, 2004.

Cole, David, and Jules Lobel. *Less Safe, Less Free: Why America Is Losing the War on Terror.* New York: New Press, 2007.

Conason, Joe. *It Can Happen Here: Authoritarian Peril in the Age of Bush.* NY: St. Martin's Press, 2007.

Dash, Samuel. *The Intruders: Unreasonable Searches and Seizures from King John to John Ashcroft.*

New Brunswick, NJ: Rutgers University Press, 2004.

Ivins, Molly, and Lou Dubose. *Bill of Wrongs: The Executive Branch's Assault on America's Fundamental Rights.* New York: Random House, 2007.

Lewis, Anthony. *Freedom for the Thought that We Hate: A Biography of the First Amendment.* New York: Basic Books, 2007.

Posner, Richard. *Not a Suicide Pact: The Constitution in a Time of National Emergency.* New York: Oxford University Press, 2006.

Rosen, Jeffrey. *The Naked Crowd: Reclaiming Security and Freedom in an Anxious Age.* New York: Random House, 2004.

Chapter 9. The War in Iraq

Bremer, L. Paul III. *My Year in Iraq: The Struggle to Build a Future of Hope.* New York: Simon & Schuster, 2006.

Baker, James A., III, and Lee H. Hamilton et al., *The Iraq Study Group Report*. New York: Vintage, 2006.

Irons, Peter. *War Powers: How the Imperial Presidency Hijacked the Constitution*. New York: Metropolitan Books, 2005.

Isikoff, Michael, and David Corn. *Hubris: The Inside Story of Spin, Scandal, and the Selling of the Iraq War*. New York: Crown Publishers, 2006.

Johnson, Chalmers. *The Sorrows of Empire: Militarism, Secrecy, and the End of the Republic*. New York: Metropolitan Books, 2004.

Lieven, Anatol. *America Right or Wrong: An Anatomy of American Nationalism*. New York: Oxford University Press, 2004.

Miller, T. Christian. *Blood Money: Wasted Billions, Lost Lives, and Corporate Greed in Iraq*. New York: Little, Brown and Company, 2006.

Pape, Robert A. *Dying to Win: The Strategic Logic of Suicide Terrorism*. New York: Random House, 2005.

Prestowitz, Clyde. *Rogue Nation: American Unilateralism and the Failure of Good Intentions*. New York: Basic Books, 2004.

Ricks, Thomas E. *Fiasco: The American Military Adventure in Iraq*. New York: Penguin, 2006.

Risen, James. *State of War: The Secret History of the CIA and the Bush Administration*. New York: Free Press, 2006.

The Bush Administration's Public Statements on Iraq. Prepared for Rep. Henry A. Waxman. *United States House of Representatives Committee on Government Reform—Minority Staff Special Investigations Division* (March 16, 2004).

Scheuer, Michael. *Marching Toward Hell: America and Islam After Iraq*. New York: Free Press, 2008.

Stiglitz, Joseph E., and Linda J. Bilmes. *The Three Million Dollar War: The True Cost of the Iraq Conflict*. New York: W.W. Norton, 2008.

Walt, Stephen M. *Taming American Power: The Global Response to U.S. Primacy*. New York: W. W. Norton, 2005.

Weiner, Tim. *Legacy of Ashes: The History of the CIA*. New York: Doubleday, 2007.

Wilson, Joseph E. *The Politics of Truth: Inside the Lies that Led to War and Betrayed My Wife's CIA Identity*. New York: Carroll & Graf, 2004.

———. "What I Didn't Find in Africa," *New York Times* (July 6, 2003).

Wilson, Valerie Plame. *Fair Game: My Life as a Spy, My Betrayal by the White House*. New York: Simon & Schuster, 2007.

Chapter 10.
The Politics of Torture

Eggen, Dan. "Justice Probes Authors Of Waterboarding Memos." *Washington Post* (February 23, 2008).

Falkoff, Marc. "Politics at Guantánamo: The Former Chief Prosecutor Speaks." *The Jurist*. Pittsburgh: University of Pittsburgh Law School, *http://jurist.law.pitt. edu/forumy/2007/11/politics-at-guantanamo-former-chief.php* (November 2, 2007).

Goldsmith, Jack. *The Terror Presidency: Law and Judgment Inside the Bush Administration.* New York: W. W. Norton, 2007.

Greenberg, Karen J., ed. *The Torture Debate in America.* New York: Cambridge University Press, 2006.

Greenberg, Karen J. and, Joshua L. Dratel, eds. *The Torture Papers: The Road to Abu Ghraib.* New York: Cambridge University Press, 2005.

Newhouse, John. *Imperial America: The Bush Assault on the World Order.* New York: Alfred A. Knopf, 2003.

Singer, Peter. *The President of Good and Evil: The Ethics of George W. Bush.* New York: Dutton, 2004.

Yoo, John. *The Powers of War and Peace: The Constitution and Foreign Affairs After 9/11.* Chicago: University of Chicago Press, 2005.

———. *War by Other Means: An Insider's Account of the War on Terror.* New York: Atlantic Monthly Press, 2006.

Chapter 11. Democracy?

Freedom House, *Freedom in the World 2007*, http://www. freedomhouse.org.

Halper, Stefan and Jonathan Clarke. *America Alone: The Neo-Conservatives and The Global Order.* New York: Cambridge University Press, 2004.

Journal of Democracy, http://www. journalofdemocracy.org.

Ottaway, Marina, and Thomas Carothers. "Think Again: Middle East Democracy," *Foreign Policy* (November–December 2004).

Parsi, Trita. *Treacherous Alliance: The Secret Dealings of Israel, Iran, and the United States.* New Haven, CT: Yale University Press, 2007.

Pearse, Meic. *Why the Rest Hates the West: Understanding the Roots of Global Rage.* Downers Grove, IL: InterVarsity Press, 2004.

Wright, Robin B. *Dreams and Shadows: The Future of the Middle East.* New York: Penguin Press, 2008.

Chapter 12. The Bush Doctrine

Arms Control Association, *Arms Control Today* at http://www. armscontrol.org/act.

Bush, George W. "National Security Strategy of the United States of America." The White House (September 17, 2002), www. whitehouse.gov/nsc/nss.pdf.

Gurtov, Mel. *Superpower on Crusade: The Bush Doctrine in U.S. Foreign Policy.* Boulder, CO: Lynne Rienner, 2006.

Kellner, Douglas. *From 9/11 to Terror War: The Dangers of the Bush Doctrine.* Lanham, MD: Rowman & Littlefield, 2003.

Ritter, Scott. *Target Iran: The Truth About the White House's Plans for*

Regime Change. New York: Nation Books, 2006.

Wirtz, James J., and James A. Russell, "U.S. Policy on Preventive War and Preemption," *The Nonproliferation Review*, 10, 1 (Spring 2003), pp. 113–123.

Chapter 13. The Bush Legacy

Cullen, Jim. *Imperfect Presidents: Tales of Misadventure and Triumph.* New York: Palgrave Macmillan, 2007.

Hirsh, Michael. *At War with Ourselves: Why America Is Squandering Its Chance to Build a Better World.* New York: Oxford University Press, 2003.

Johnson, Chalmers. *Nemesis: The Last Days of the American Republic.* New York: Metropolitan Books, 2006.

Kaplan, Fred. *Daydream Believers: How a Few Grand Ideas Wrecked American Power.* Hoboken, NJ: John Wiley & Sons, 2008.

Murphy, Cullen. *Are We Rome? The Fall of an Empire and the Fate of America.* Boston: Houghton Mifflin, 2007.

Oliphant, Thomas. *Utter Incompetents: Ego and Ideology in the Age of Bush.* New York: Thomas Dunne Books, St. Martin's Press, 2007.

Ross, Dennis. *Statecraft: And How to Restore America's Standing in the World.* New York: Farrar, Straus, and Giroux, 2007.

Unger, Craig. *The Fall of the House of Bush: The Untold Story of How a Band of True Believers Seized the Executive Branch, Started the Iraq War, and Still Imperils America's Future.* New York: Scribner, 2007.

About the Authors

Jim Morin is the acclaimed Pulitzer Prize–winning editorial cartoonist for the *Miami Herald*. He won the Pulitzer in 1996, shared the prize with the *Miami Herald* Editorial Board in 1983, and was a finalist in 1977 and 1990. Most recently he won the prestigious Herblock Prize in 2007. Morin is the author of three books: *Famous Cats*, *Jim Morin's Field Guide to Birds*, and a collection of political cartoons, *Line of Fire*. His cartoons and oil paintings have been exhibited in galleries and museums worldwide. Morin's cartoons are distributed internationally by Cartoonists and Writers/New York Times Syndicate.

Walter C. Clemens, Jr. is Professor of Political Science at Boston University and Associate, Harvard University Davis Center for Russian and Eurasian Studies. He is the author of *America and the World, 1898–2025: Achievements, Failures, Alternative Futures* (2000) and a dozen other books including the highly praised *Dynamics of International Relations*, 2nd ed. (2004). His op-eds have appeared in the *Christian Science Monitor*, *Los Angeles Times*, *New York Times*, *Wall Street Journal*, and *Washington Post*. Clemens has been a consultant to the U.S. Department of State, Institute for Defense Analyses, and U.S. Arms Control and Disarmament Agency.